SUPER FUN SCIENCE

Multisensory Object Talks
from the Psalms

by Heno Head, Jr.

Standard PUBLISHING

Cincinnati, Ohio

Published by Standard Publishing, Cincinnati, Ohio
www.standardpub.com

Printed in: United States of America
Project editors: Elaina Meyers, Rosemary H. Mitchell
Illustration: Rusty Fletcher
Cover and interior design: Sandra S. Wimmer
Interior production: Dale Meyers
Author photo, back cover: John Morton

ISBN 978-0-7847-2971-7

Library of Congress Cataloging-in-Publication Data

Head, Heno.
  Super fun science / Heno Head, Jr.
    p. cm.
  ISBN 978-0-7847-2971-7
  1. Bible. O.T. Psalms--Study and teaching (Elementary) 2. Science--Miscellanea--Study and teaching (Elementary) I. Title.
  BS1430.55.H425 2011
  223'.2007--dc22
                          2011010163

16 15 14 13 12 11   1 2 3 4 5 6 7 8 9

Dedication

To my father, who truly enjoyed his walk with God.

Foreword

The book of Psalms in the Bible is one of the most outstanding pieces of literature in the world. Many of the psalms are so visual one not only reads them but "sees" them as well. After reading through the Psalms some 30 times, the single phrase that most often comes to my mind is, "It's all about God." The "It" would be the book of Psalms, the Bible, and life itself. Our very existence is all about God.

David, who wrote most of the psalms, had a special relationship with God. There were times he was so close to God, David could barely contain his joy. That joy naturally spilled over into his writing.

Now here we are 3,000 years later, still seeking closeness to God. We discover that the richness of the psalms is as relevant today as ever. *Super Fun Science* has been written to help us convey to our children the joy of the Lord as it is found throughout the book of Psalms. Our life does indeed become super and fun when God is at the center. David would say "Amen" to that.

Safety

Most demos in this book are intended for adults to lead. Specific instructions are provided for those demos in which child participation is safe and appropriate.

All demos have been tested as written in this book. If you make any adjustments, be sure to test them before doing your presentation. Use good judgment when using or adapting any of these demos.

While Standard Publishing grants permission to alter and adapt these demos, Standard Publishing claims no liability or responsibility for the content of any such adaptations.

Preparation

Most of the demos in this book can be prepared quickly and supplies easily obtained. However, some do require advance preparation. Look for this handy icon so you will know at a glance which demos need more time to prepare.

CD

The CD contains the entire text of the book. Use the CD to:

- e-mail demos to leaders.
- print patterns and illustrations as needed.
- have a complete, backup copy of everything in the book.

Table of Contents

Title   **Page**

I'm Predicting It's Addicting (Psalm 1:1, 2) 9
Floatin' Fruit (Psalm 1:3) 11
The Chaff's in a Draft (Psalm 1:4) 13
Strainer Things Have Happened (Psalm 3:3) 15
Now Hear This (Psalm 4:3) 17
Better Glad than Mad (Psalm 4:4) 19
Be Brave in the Cave (Psalm 4:6) 21
Bendable Bones (Psalm 6:2, 3) 23
High and Lifted Up (Psalm 8:1) 25
Did You See What I Saw? (Psalm 8:2) 27
From Mars to the Stars (Psalm 8:3, 4) 29
Blue Who? (Psalm 8:6-8) 31
The Choir Has the Fire (Psalm 9:1, 2) 33
Wind Tunnel in a Funnel (Psalm 10:4) 35
Having a Ball (Psalm 16:2) 37
May "Eye" Help You? (Psalm 17:8) 39
Wind-Wind Situation (Psalm 18:10) 41
Static in the Attic (Psalm 18:12) 43
Star-Spangled Angle (Psalm 19:1) 45
Whack-a-Stack (Psalm 23:1) 47
Hooping It Up (Psalm 23:3) 49
Bowl and Arrow (Psalm 23:5) 51
Falling in Love (Psalm 23:6) 53
Clean Pure Through (Psalm 24:3, 4) 55
Going Green (Psalm 25:4, 5) 57
Color My World (Psalm 27:1) 59
Getting in Shape (Psalm 28:8) 61
God Is Good All the Time (Psalm 31:19) 63
Standing for the Lord (Psalm 33:11) 65
What's Up with the Cups? (Psalm 34:3) 67

Chase the Taste (Psalm 34:8) **69**

Spectacular Binoculars (Psalm 34:8) **71**

Be Like the One You Like (Psalm 35:10) **73**

As High as the Sky (Psalm 36:5) **75**

Mountains of Fountains (Psalm 36:9) **77**

The Air up There (Psalm 37:4) **79**

Steppin' Out (Psalm 37:23) **81**

Weight for the Lord (Psalm 37:34) **83**

Blur and a Whir (Psalm 39:12) **85**

The Domino Effect (Psalm 40:8) **87**

Deep Calls to Deep (Psalm 42:7) **89**

Disappearing Engineering (Psalm 44:8) **91**

Soft Pop (Psalm 46:6,10) **93**

Air Chair (Psalm 47:8) **95**

Chair Spin Curve (Psalm 48:12-14) **97**

Time to Wash Up (Psalm 51:7) **99**

The Circle Won't Be Broken (Psalm 51:10) **101**

Shelter in the Storm (Psalm 55:8) **103**

Trust Is a Must (Psalm 56:3, 4) **105**

Leaning on Jesus (Psalm 62:3) **107**

Park Your Marker (Psalm 62:7) **109**

But First, the Thirst (Psalm 63:1) **111**

Spring into Missions (Psalm 67:1, 2) **113**

Diaper Diamonds (Psalm 68:14) **115**

But Will It Fly? (Psalm 71:17) **117**

His Grip Won't Slip (Psalm 73:23) **119**

Near and Dear (Psalm 73:28) **121**

Banana Hamma (Psalm 78:9, 10) **123**

Lettuce Be Strong (Psalm 78:10) **125**

Slo-Mo Flow (Psalm 78:15, 16) **127**

It's Raining Grain (Psalm 78:24, 25) **129**

Penny for Your Thoughts (Psalm 78:70, 71) **131**

Fun and Done (Psalm 84:10) **133**

Meet in the Middle (Psalm 86:15) **135**

Where Did the Song Go Wrong? (Psalm 88:13) **137**

Deep and Wide (Psalm 92:5) **139**

Don't Mope over the Soap (Psalm 95:7, 8) **141**

Zingy Thingy (Psalm 96:11, 12) **143**

East to West, Least to Best (Psalm 103:12) **145**

Riding the Wind (Psalm 104:3) **147**

Don't Take It Lion Down (Psalm 104:21) **149**

Working for Peanuts (Psalm 104:25) **151**

Twist of Faith (Psalm 105:8) **153**

Bob the Prophet (Psalm 105:15) **155**

F.R.O.G. (Psalm 105:30) **157**

Wave on Wave (Psalm 107:25, 26) **159**

Don't Stress, Just Bless (Psalm 109:17) 161

Dial Me Up, Scotty (Psalm 113:3) 163

Gotta Hand It to You (Psalm 118:16) 165

Pyramid of Prayer (Psalm 118:28) 167

Things of Wonder (Psalm 119:18) 169

Life Preserver (Psalm 119:25, 37, 40) 171

Promises, Promises (Psalm 119:41) 173

Sweeeet! (Psalm 119:47) 175

Pouring Air (Psalm 119:62) 177

Bowled Over (Psalm 119:68) 179

The Big Dig (Psalm 119:72) 181

Out to Launch (Psalm 119:120) 183

The Gift of a Lift (Psalm 121:1, 2) 185

Oh, Boy. We've Got Joy! (Psalm 126:3) 187

The Will to Build (Psalm 127:1) 189

March of the Starch (Psalm 128:1) 191

The Karo Pharaoh (Psalm 135:9) 193

Bubblin' Up (Psalm 138:1) 195

Above All Things (Psalm 138:2) 197

Talk About Fast (Psalm 139:10) 199

Hey, It's in Our DNA (Psalm 139:13) 201

Sands of the Seashore (Psalm 139:17, 18) 203

Twinkie, Twinkie, Little Pinky (Psalm 141:8) 205

May the Butter Man Win (Psalm 143:10) 207

Rolling on Level Ground (Psalm 143:10) 209

Smoke on the Mountain (Psalm 144:5) 211

The Key to Victory (Psalm 144:9, 10) 213

Wham! (Psalm 150:1, 3-5) 215

Topical Index 218

Introduction

Research consistently proves that people remember 10% of what they hear, 20% of what they see, 50% of what they see and hear, and 90% of what they see, hear, and do. With this knowledge and with the demos presented in this book, you can be a powerful influence in the lives of young people. Not only will you teach kids about the book of Psalms, you will involve all of their senses to help them remember God's Word like never before.

This book contains 104 all-new object talks, each based on a simple science demonstration. The demos are all organized in the following manner:

Title of the demo

Scripture reference or thought from the Psalms

What's Gonna Happen—a brief summary of the demo

The How Behind the Wow—an explanation of the science principle for the demo

What You Need—a list of materials necessary for the demo

What You Do—instructions on how to practice and perform the demo

What You Say—the talk itself, written in Heno Head's conversational, humorous style. Though you certainly could read this text right from the book, it would be more personal if you were familiar enough with it to make it your own.

Whether you use these talks in Sunday school, children's church, the children's sermon, youth groups, clubs, or at home, the demos you do and the words you say will capture young hearts and minds for Christ.

I'm Predicting It's Addicting

Psalm 1:1, 2
Blessed is the one who does not walk in step with the wicked or stand in the way that sinners take or sit in the company of mockers, but whose delight is in the law of the LORD, and who meditates on his law day and night.

What's Gonna Happen
You're going to pop some Bubble Wrap®.

The How Behind the Wow
Boyle's law states that in an enclosed container of gas, the more pressure from without, the less space the container takes up. Each bubble is an enclosed container, and you're bringing the pressure to bear until . . .

What You Need
Scissors
Bubble Wrap with large bubbles (sold as a roll in the tape/mailer section at Walmart)

What You Do
1. Use the scissors to cut out a couple of Bubble Wrap sections, each about a foot square. Be sure you have the large bubbles.
2. Practice with these squares, then cut out two more for your program.
3. Have the Bubble Wrap out of sight as you begin your talk.
4. That's it. Oh . . . have fun.

What You Say

(You need to be standing, holding the Bubble Wrap out of sight.)

Today we're going to talk about addictions—those pesky, little habits that grow on us. Addictions come in all sizes and shapes. They could be anything from food to TV to sports to shopping. And, of course, some addictions are way serious. None of us wants to go there. Maybe you've seen TV ads for substance-abuse recovery programs.

But, I'll tell you what, of all the addictions out there, no one ever talks about the quickest, slickest addiction of all . . . *(whip out)* Bubble Wrap! Yes, indeed, kids, there they sit . . . those little air-filled bubbles just waiting to be popped. If you listen closely, you can even hear them going *(high-pitched voice)*, "Pop me, pop me." But don't go there. If you're bopping along and see Bubble Wrap lying on a table, just keep on bopping. 'Cause if you're not careful, you may go from bopping to stopping. While you're stopping, you start going, "Hmm." That "hmm" is the sound of trouble. For you'll go from Bop to Stop to Drop.

(Sit in chair.)

There you sit. Before you know it, you pick up that Bubble Wrap, feel those little air-filled packs of pleasure just waiting to be . . . Uh-huh, you guessed it. You go from Bop to Stop to Drop and finally . . . *(Pop one.)* Oh, no . . . to Pop! And there you go. *(Pop 4 or 5.)* Oh, it feels good to pop those bubbles. *(Twist the sheet and machine gun them.)* And see, you're hooked. Gotta have that Bubble Wrap. Give me more or I'm out the door.

Now the thing is, long before my little story about Bubble Wrap, King David wrote the following words in Psalm 1. He said, "Blessed is the one who does not *walk,* as in Bop, in step with the wicked or *stand,* as in Stop, in the way that sinners take or *sit,* as in Drop, in the company of mockers." See, same steps as today. Back then: Walk. Stand. Sit. Today: Bop. Stop. Drop.

But David goes on to say in verse two, "but whose delight is in the law of the LORD and who meditates on his law day and night." Meditating on God's Word. Now there's a sweet addiction. So, in conclusion, kids, when temptation comes along, just keep on BOPPING so you won't be *(hold up new piece of Bubble Wrap, but fight the temptation and set it down easy)* POPPING.

Floatin' Fruit

Psalm 1:3

That person is like a tree planted by streams of water, which yields its fruit in season and whose leaf does not wither—whatever they do prospers.

What's Gonna Happen

You will put some fruit into water for a sink-or-swim test.

The How Behind the Wow

One of the key properties of matter is density. Water's density is 1 g/mL. Objects that are less dense than one gram/milliliter will float; greater than one gram/milliliter will sink. Many fruits, because of the air in either the fruit itself or the peels, will float.

What You Need

Aquarium or medium-size plastic tub
Water
Fruit (apple, orange, lemon, strawberry, grape, banana)
Bible

What You Do

1. Fill the aquarium or plastic tub with enough water to test the fruits.
2. Put the fruit in for their sink-or-swim tests.
3. That's it. Take out and store fruit in fridge. Have aquarium ready to go for your talk.
4. Keep fruit out of sight until indicated in talk.

What You Say

Do you see what I have here today? That's right. An aquarium *(or a plastic tub)*. And it has in it? Right again. Good ol' H_2O. That's what science-type folks like us call water. So I've got a tub and I've got water, so what's next? Well, what's next is—swimming. And after that, how about—drumroll—the Bible! *(Hold out your Bible.)* Yes, indeed, the Bible.

I've got a verse from the book of Psalms, the very first psalm to be exact. Psalm 1:3 says that a believer "is like a tree planted by streams of water, which yields its fruit in season."

How about that? Those of us who are believers will produce fruit for the Lord. In his time and season. You don't know what type of orchard you'll produce. Maybe you'll be a missionary to another country, the first person to take the gospel to a tribe of people living there. Or maybe you'll be a Christian singer. Or a preacher. Or a doctor for the Lord. And the list goes on. You don't know, but his promise is that you will produce much fruit. That means you will influence many people for the kingdom.

So about that swimming. I've got six fruits here. *(Show fruit.)* Thought what we'd do is put them in the water one at a time and see if they sink or swim. With each fruit you get to make your sink-or-swim call ahead of time. Here we go. Apple. What do you think, sink or swim? Okay, we'll see. *(Set apple in water.)* Good call. Now . . . *(proceed with the others, fairly rapidly).*

(When finished . . .) And so, just like we had different types of fruit for our sink-or-swim test today, remember that God has different pathways planned for each of your lives. And on those pathways he has great things planned for you to do. Someday, maybe someday very soon, you will begin bearing much fruit for his kingdom. And all you do will prosper.

The Chaff's in a Draft

Psalm 1:4

Not so the wicked! They are like chaff that the wind blows away.

What's Gonna Happen

You're going to blow foam chips with a hair dryer.

The How Behind the Wow

This is a density demo. The foam chips are so lightweight they are easily blown by the wind of the hair dryer. The glass stones are too heavy to be blown around.

What You Need

Flat pan or board

Styrofoam™ cup

Extension cord (optional)

10 glass stones or small rocks

Hair dryer

Bible

What You Do

1. Place the pan upside down.
2. Set the glass stones or rocks on the pan.
3. Break the cup into chips, then sprinkle 15–20 of the foam chips among the stones.
4. From a distance of some three feet, blow the hair dryer down onto the pan. Start on low speed, which may be all you need.
5. After the chips blow away, gradually get closer with the hair dryer. If not on high already, do so now. Get within a foot of the pan.
6. That's it. Have everything ready, but plan on starting from scratch (empty pan) for your talk.

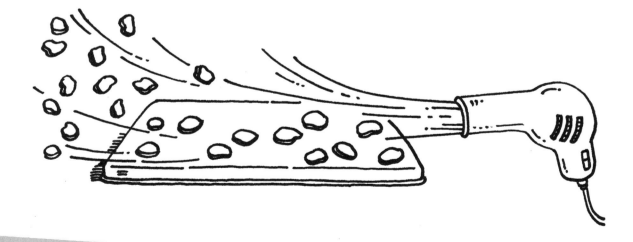

What You Say

I've got a verse for you today. It's talking about the bad guys out there. The verse is Psalm 1:4. Before I read it, I have to give you just a little background. Verse three talks about the believers in God. It says that the believers will be like trees planted by streams of water. They will produce much fruit for God. Whatever they do will prosper. Then comes verse four. It says, "Not so the wicked! They are like chaff that the wind blows away."

What is chaff? Does anybody know? *(Accept any answers. Someone may get it right, but if not . . .)* On top of wheat stalks are the little wheat seeds. These are good things. Around the seeds, though, are tiny, flaky, lightweight papery husks. These little husks are known as chaff. In movies you see people throwing the grain up in the air and letting it hit a flat screen. What they're doing is knocking off the chaff and letting the wind blow it away. You see, they want the seeds for making bread, but they don't want the chaff.

That's the way it is with people who ignore God. In their own minds these people think they're big deals, but really they're just lightweight chaff—no tree by the water, no fruit, no spiritual prosperity. You and I don't want to go there. We want to be God's children. Kind of like what I've got today.

First, I'll set out my pan. Now, I'll put on some glass stones *(or rocks)*. Those are like us; trying to do the right thing for the Lord. Next, I'll sprinkle on a little chaff *(sprinkle chips slowly)* in the form of these foam chips. These are the bad guys, with no time for God.

All we need now is a little wind. Ah-ha, how about this hair dryer? *(Use low speed.)* Let's see who handles the wind. Whoa, would you look at that? It's chips ahoy. The wind is barely going and already the chaff is blowing away, just like the verse says. *(Hair dryer off.)* So remember, don't get blown away like chaff. Stand strong in the Lord's power.

Strainer Things Have Happened

Psalm 3:3
But you, LORD, are a shield around me, my glory, the One who lifts my head high.

What's Gonna Happen
You will shield hole-punch dots from static electricity.

The How Behind the Wow
Rubbing a balloon creates static electricity, a buildup of electrons. These electrons will attract paper punch-outs, causing them to jump to the balloon. The metal of the strainer will function as a shield, dispersing the electricity.

What You Need
2 balloons

Paper

Hole punch or scissors

Small metal strainer, such as a tea strainer

Cloth (wool is best, but any will do)

Resealable plastic bag

What You Do
1. Inflate and tie off a balloon. Inflate it tightly.
2. Punch or cut out some 20 paper dots.
3. Set the paper dots on a table.
4. Rub the balloon with the cloth, giving the balloon a static charge.
5. Lower the balloon near the dots. They will leap—yes, leap, not dawdle, but leap—upward. You are a scientist!
6. Do the whole demo a second time, with the only difference being that you set the strainer down over the dots.
7. This time when you place the balloon down near the dots, they are unaffected by the static electrical charge. The strainer absorbs the electricity, thus shielding the paper dots.
8. As they say, you're good to go. Store the paper dots in the plastic bag. You should inflate a fresh balloon just before your talk.

What You Say

Let's talk about God. We're going to do a one-word thing, as in give me one word that says something about God. Are you ready? So let's start. What is one word that comes to your mind when you think of God? *(Encourage any answers.)* Okay, good. Love. Creation. Father. Eternal. Forgiveness.

Here's one *(in case no one said it)* . . . protection. God is our unseen protector in so many ways. David talks about this in Psalm 3:3. In that verse he says, "But you, LORD, are a shield around me." You get the picture, and it really is a picture—God, over and around us, protecting us in ways we'll never know, at least on this side of eternity. If there is anyone who has your best interests at heart, it is your heavenly Father.

Reminds me of this balloon. Normally a balloon means fun and happy times. On this occasion, though, the balloon is bringing stress into the lives of these paper dots. Let me show you what I mean. I'll just set the dots on the table here. The dots represent us, and the balloon stands for too much static in our lives. Like this. *(Rub balloon and static up the dots.)* See what I mean? We're just trying to get along, but we can't concentrate because of the nutso balloon. Actually looks pretty cool, though, doesn't it?

So what we need is a shield around us. Some protection, just like Psalm 3:3 talks about: "But you, LORD, are a shield around me." And, ta-da, we have that shield. It's this strainer. The strainer is made out of metal, which is a good thing. Watch closely. I'll bunch all the dots together—all of us together—and I'll set the strainer down over us. Now let's static up the balloon *(rub good)* and lower the stress in our direction. Watch the dots closely, okay? See, they aren't moving. They are totally unaffected by the static in the attic.

So it is with us, my friends. For you see, it can be revealed that we have the shield—the shield of protection from our heavenly Father.

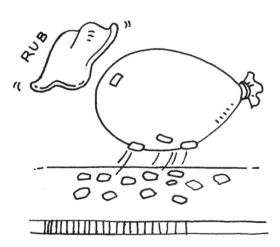

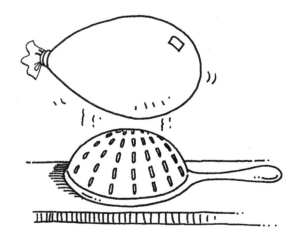

Now Hear This

Psalm 4:3b
The LORD hears when I call to him.

What's Gonna Happen
You'll make a cone to help you hear a ticking timer.

The How Behind the Wow
Most of our ear is actually inside the head. The outer ear is primarily to help funnel sounds to our middle and inner ear. Sometimes you'll see people helping the outer ear by cupping a hand to the ear and wheezing, "What's that you say, sonny?" In this demo, a rolled-up cone will take the place of the hand.

What You Need
Poster board
Timer that ticks
Tape
Scissors

What You Do
1. Roll the poster board into a cone shape. Do this by starting the roll at a corner. Keep this corner small, maybe the diameter of a baseball. The other end of the cone should flare out closer to basketball size.
2. Tape the cone to hold its shape.
3. You will need to use the scissors to level the ends of the cone.
4. Start the timer ticking. Set it on a table. Hold the cone to your ear, small end near your head, and find the timer by listening for the ticking. Intentionally face the wrong way and work toward the timer.
5. In your presentation you will have a child find the timer.

What You Say

The word *hear* appears in the Psalms more than 55 times. A main way the word is used comes when the writer asks God to hear our prayers. Along this line we get verses like Psalm 4:3. That verse says, "The LORD hears when I call to him." And do you know what? Not only did the Lord hear them back in Bible days, he hears us when we call to him. You and I may have good hearing, but it can't touch God's hearing. He can hear the quietest sound; even the gentlest heartbeat.

With that in mind, today I have a hearing test for someone. It has to do with this giant cone. *(Show.)* You see most of our actual hearing is done inside the ear. The outer part of the ear that we see is mainly to help direct sounds down our ear canal. Have you ever seen an older person cup her hand to an ear? *(Illustrate.)* What she's doing is using her hand to catch more of the sound waves. Our cone should catch a whole lot of sound waves, shouldn't it?

The sound we'll be using comes from this timer. Here, I'll wind it up and show you how it sounds. *(Do this.)* Everybody hear that ticking? Good. I need a volunteer. *(Select someone.)* Hold the big cone to your ear. With your eyes closed I want you to use the cone to see if you can locate the timer. After you close your eyes I will set the timer somewhere nearby. Your job is to listen for the ticking and see if you can find the timer. Got it? Okay, here we go.

(When the timer has been located . . .) What a great job! You basically set the cone right down on the timer. Excellent work. And that reminds me just how excellent God's hearing is. Like David, we can be confident that, "The LORD hears when I call to him."

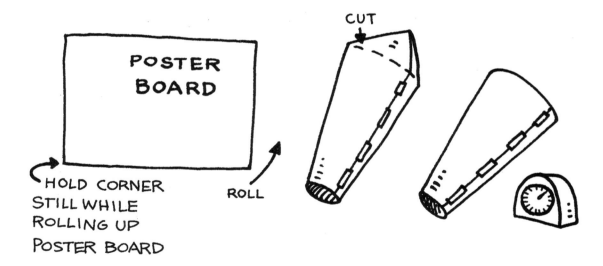

Better Glad than Mad

Psalm 4:4
Tremble and do not sin; when you are on your beds, search your hearts and be silent.

What's Gonna Happen
You will drive three nails partially into a board, then pull them out.

The How Behind the Wow
Let's see . . . hammer, nails, wood. Is this a construction project or science thing, or both? Hey, here's a thought. The hammer is a third-class lever when driving in the nails; a first-class lever when pulling them out.

What You Need
Hammer
2 small blocks of wood (1 x 4, 2 x 4, etc.)
Smaller block of wood for pivot point when removing the nails
6 nails
Marker

What You Do
1. Set out a block of wood. Draw three hearts on one side. Space these hearts out a bit.
2. Drive three nails into the wood, one nail into each heart. The nails should go in about a half-inch.
3. Place the smaller block near the nails to use as a lever to help pull the nails out.
4. You're ready. Either turn the board over for your talk or use the second board. Draw three new hearts. When doing your talk, don't necessarily call attention to the hearts. If the kids should see them, fine. If not, better.
5. If you bent any nails, replace them for your talk.

What You Say

Today's subject is anger. Do you ever get mad either at things, or people, or situations, or just life? Maybe you don't get your way, or someone upsets you. The list goes on.

From time to time, possibly all of us get mad. But let's try not to get mad, okay? Let's really, really, did I mention—*really*—try not to get angry, especially at other people. Words we say to them, or they say to us, can last a long, long time.

Psalm 4:4 puts it this way: "Tremble and do not sin; when you are on your beds, search your hearts and be silent." You see we can get so upset during the day that we end up taking it with us at night when we go to sleep. Instead of doing that, let's learn to search our heart, pray to God, give the situation to him, and relax. It will help keep us from hurting anyone with our words.

I'll show you what I mean. I've got a board here and three nails. I'm going to drive these nails into the board. Each nail is like a time we get mad at someone and say something we later wish we could take back. Those hurtful things we say are like emotional nails—not real steel nails like these, but words that wound the other person's heart.

So here we go. Temper tantrum number one coming up. *(Drive in nail one.)* Then later, when we didn't get our way, "Squawk, squawk, squawk." *(Drive in nail two.)* Finally, just when we needed rest, we instead got stress and . . . *(Drive in nail three.)*

Later we may think, *Why did I do and say those things?* We may even go back and tell each person, "Sorry" *(pull nail one)*, "Excuse me" *(pull nail two)*, "My bad" *(pull nail three)*. That makes things better, no doubt. But, kids *(hold board toward them so that they see the three nail holes left behind in the hearts)*, things may never quite be the same.

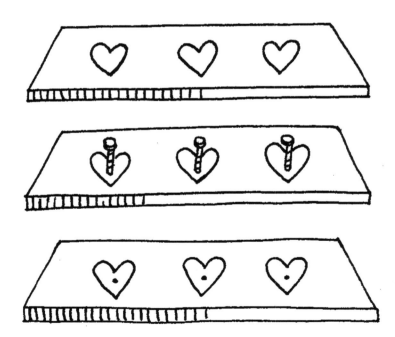

Be Brave in the Cave

Psalm 4:6b; 57 (intro)

Let the light of your face shine on us . . . (Of David. When he had fled from Saul into the cave.)

What's Gonna Happen

You will make a shoe box cave, then shine a light into it.

The How Behind the Wow

The light you'll be shining is a glow stick. This is made of two tubes—an outer plastic one and an inner glass tube. Each contains a different chemical, one of which is often hydrogen peroxide. When the glow stick is bent, the glass tube breaks and the two chemicals mix. The chemical reaction produces light without heat. This type of reaction is known as chemiluminescence.

What You Need

Shoe box with lid
Scissors
Glue
Steak knife
Tape

2 glow sticks (available in toy sections or some outdoor sections of stores; yellow works best, if possible)
Copy of pictures from this demo

What You Do

1. Use the steak knife to cut a small, horizontal window (1" x 2") in one end of the shoe box. Save this window cutout for step 2.
2. In the shoe box lid, cut out a small postage stamp-size square. This square should be midway along and toward one side of the box. Use the tape as a hinge to place your window cutout over this square.
3. Make a copy of the three pictures with this demo. Cut out the pictures and glue them inside the shoe box. Put one picture on each wall—baby Jesus to the left of the window, Bible straight ahead, cross to the right. Or just draw them with a marker inside the shoe box.
4. Be sure the lid is on the box. Look through the window into your box. Hopefully, it is fairly difficult to see the three pictures.
5. To activate one of the glow sticks, take it out of its package and bend till the inner glass breaks. After this happens, shake the stick. Open the window cutout and insert the glow stick straight downward. Hold the glow stick while checking to see if you can see the pictures.
6. Depending on how near your practice time is to your presentation time, you may be able to use the same glow stick. Otherwise, you have a backup. Either way, you're good to glow.

What You Say

I saw an interesting thing in the book of Psalms recently. Oftentimes above a psalm there will be a note. The note will tell who wrote the Psalm, plus maybe a little other information. Above Psalm 57 it says, "Of David. When he had fled from Saul into the cave." That made me think, *Hmm, things weren't always easy for David.* Caves are the same today as they were back then—cold, rocky, and, above all, dark.

With that in mind I just happen to have a cave today. *(Show shoebox.)* I've even cut a window in one end so we can look into the cave. Would someone like to look into the cave? Good, check it out. Dark, huh? That's pretty much all David could see too, in his cave.

What David needed was a night-light. That brings to mind Psalm 4:6, "Let the light of your face shine on us." That's something we all need, whether in a cave or not. In honor of the light of God's face, I've got this light. *(Show glow stick out of package.)* It's a light stick. I'm going to break it. *(Do so.)* Chemicals are mixing, and look! We have light. If David had been able to use a light stick back in his day, he could have written Psalm 57 in that cave at midnight.

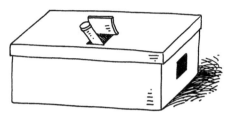

I'll put the glow stick into our shoe box. Now let's take another look inside our cave *(get your volunteer)* and see what's there. *(As the child looks in box . . .)* Since David was the great ancestor of Jesus, I've put three pictures on the wall of our cave. Those pictures are about the life of Jesus. They start on your left and go around the walls. Can you see them? Good. Tell us what you see. Baby Jesus in a manger. That's right. A Bible. In Jesus' day they wrote on scrolls. Great. And finally? Yes, a cross.

And there we have our story about David being brave in the cave. We also have three of the main things from the life of Jesus—the manger of his birth, the Word of God in his life, and his death upon the cross. His death was for you and me. The light of the Lord sure is a great thing, isn't it?

Bendable Bones

Psalm 6:2, 3
Have mercy on me, LORD, for I am faint; heal me, LORD, for my bones are in agony. My soul is in deep anguish. How long, LORD, how long?

What's Gonna Happen
You will soak a chicken bone in vinegar until the bone becomes rubbery.

The How Behind the Wow
Bones contain the mineral calcium. Vinegar is diluted acetic acid. When the bone is allowed to soak in vinegar for several days, the acid dissolves all the calcium. Without the calcium, the bone becomes soft and flexible.

What You Need
Jar with lid or butter tub with lid
Vinegar
Chicken bone (small wishbones take 2–3 days; drumsticks take a week or so)
Resealable plastic bag

What You Do
1. Like the Chick-fil-A® cows say, "Eat Mor Chikin," then save the bones.
2. Clean the chicken bones well.
3. Pour vinegar into your container.
4. Place the cleaned chicken bone(s) into the vinegar.
5. Put the lid on the container.
6. Wait. If you need a demo for church tomorrow, you're on the wrong page.
7. Check the bones every two or three days. Also, it's not a bad idea to change the vinegar on those check days.
8. When the bones are rubbery, you will be able to bend them till opposite ends touch, without an accompanying *snap!* For the drumstick, this is right at seven days.
9. Use soap and water to wash off the vinegar. Store the chicken bones in a resealable plastic bag. Use just a little water to keep the bones moist.

What You Say

King David wrote most of the psalms. One thing about his writing—he wrote the way he felt. Which is not a bad idea when it comes to writing. If he felt happy, he wrote about joy. If he felt deeply spiritual, he wrote beautiful words like the twenty-third psalm. When he felt as if his enemies were closing in on him, he wrote psalms that bristled with warfare.

Then there are times when he wrote hurting psalms. He was just hurting, that's all we can say. Have you ever been there? If so, you know how David felt. Maybe he was on to something, expressing his feelings by writing them down. That's what he did in Psalm 6. Listen to verses two and three: "Have mercy on me, LORD, for I am faint; heal me, LORD, for my bones are in agony. My soul is in deep anguish. How long, LORD, how long?"

David was hurting in body and soul. His bones were in agony and his soul in anguish. Mercy. But here's the key—he took it to God. That's what he was doing even as he was writing. It was as if David were writing a prayer.

So let's talk about his bones being in agony. That doesn't sound like fun. *(Hold up bone.)* I just happen to have a bone here; a chicken bone actually. Can you tell what kind of bone it is? You're right, a drumstick *(or other)*. That bone doesn't look to be in agony, does it? Not even close. But watch this. *(Bend bone.)* How about that? And it springs right back in place when I let it go.

David may have been in agony, but his bones never did bend like that. So if you ever see a chicken bone bent double, think about David writing his hurting prayer to God. If we ever have those hurting times, let's do what David did—take them to the Lord in prayer.

VINEGAR

High and Lifted Up

Psalm 8:1a
LORD, our Lord, how majestic is your name in all the earth!

What's Gonna Happen
You're going to hover a balloon with a hair dryer.

The How Behind the Wow
Bernoulli's principle states that the faster a fluid (air/liquid) flows, the less pressure it exerts on surfaces it moves past. The balloon hovers in the fast-flowing air stream because the still air out to the sides has greater pressure. This greater pressure is pushing inward, keeping the balloon steady.

What You Need
2–12" yellow balloons
3 paper clips
Hair dryer
Permanent marker

What You Do
1. Inflate and tie off the balloon.
2. Hold the balloon so that the knot is at the bottom. Write GOD in large letters on the balloon.
3. Turn the hair dryer on low. Point it so that the air flow is upward.
4. Place the balloon in the air flow. The balloon hovers so easily you may need to add two or three paper clips at the bottom for ballast.
5. As the balloon hovers in the air, you're announcing to all the world that the name of God is high and lifted up—in other words, majestic.
6. Now tilt the hair dryer slightly to the side. The balloon will go with the air flow. After a bit, tilt it back to the other side. Again, the balloon follows along. Bernoulli's principle is pretty neat and sweet.
7. That's it. You may need to inflate and label a fresh balloon on the day of your presentation.

What You Say

As a believer in God, do you know that there is one thing you can never do too much? It's true. No matter how hard you try you can never do this one thing too much. And that is . . . honor God's name! He himself exalted his own name above all things, so when we do the same thing, we are doing a really good thing.

Here, I'll show you what I mean. I just happen to have a balloon with a name on it. Everybody know whose name that is? You're right, it's God's name . . . in big letters, I might add. Seeing God's name on the balloon brings to mind this verse from Psalm 8:1: "LORD, our Lord, how majestic is your name in all the earth!" Isn't that an excellent verse? And it ends with an exclamation point. David is flying high as he is pumping up God's name.

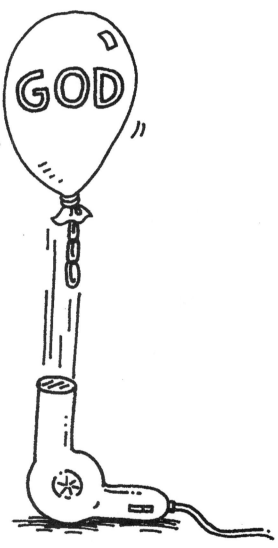

I think we should fly high too, as we pump up God's name. That's why I brought this hair dryer. Check this out as we give God's name a lift. *(Turn hair dryer on low and hover the balloon. Talk over the hair dryer.)* See how we're lifting up God's name? I think he loves it when his children honor his name. We don't mistreat his name or use it lightly. Instead we honor it by the way we live and speak and do for others. And, by the way, I'm one of his children too, even at my age.

Hopefully, if you and I honor God's name, then people over here *(tilt dryer to one side)* will begin to honor God's name too. Then, if they do, maybe people back over here *(tilt dryer to other side)* will start honoring God's name as well. It will become contagious. We'll *all* honor God's name in everything we do.

So remember *(turn off hair dryer, let balloon come down for a landing),* it's like Psalm 8:1 says . . . God's name is majestic in all the earth.

Did You See What I Saw?

Psalm 8:2
Through the praise of children and infants
you have established a stronghold against your
enemies, to silence the foe and the avenger.

What's Gonna Happen
You will make a hanging seesaw from a ruler and clothespins.

The How Behind the Wow
Torque is a twisting force. With a lever or seesaw, we can get a relative idea of the amount of torque being produced on each side of the fulcrum. Multiply the force by the distance from the fulcrum. Suppose you hung two clothespins at a distance of two units (inches) from the fulcrum. Two times two would give you a torque of four. If you had only one clothespin to balance the other side, you could say 1 x 4 and you would know to put the one clothespin four inches distance from the fulcrum.

What You Need
2 rulers, 1 with a center hole   Yarn or string
Spring-loaded clothespins   Duct tape
Scissors   Chair

What You Do
1. Tape one of the rulers onto the chair back. This ruler should not stick out from the front or back, but off to one side, like a diving board.
2. Cut a 12-inch piece of yarn.
3. Tie one end of the yarn through the middle hole of the second ruler.
4. Make a loop in the other end of the yarn. Loop this over the "diving board" ruler. The loop should be near the end of the ruler away from the chair. Tape yarn into place with a small piece of duct tape.
5. The second ruler should hang level. You may need a tiny piece of tape for this. Each inch of this ruler is now a unit. Clip a clothespin two inches (two units) away from the fulcrum (center). It doesn't matter which side you choose.
6. Now clip a second clothespin onto the bottom of the first clothespin.
7. The ruler will definitely tilt far down to that side.
8. On the other end of the ruler, clip one clothespin four inches away from the fulcrum. The ruler will exactly balance.
9. This opens up a number of balancing possibilities. Experiment a bit. The one we'll use is: four clothespins at three units away on one side of the ruler; two clothespins at six units away on the other.
10. Go forth and see what David saw. You will either need to take things as assembled, or reset at your program location.

What You Say

You know something? You are special—to your parents, to the church, and to God. You may recall that Jesus always had time for children. And in the book of Psalms, years before Jesus lived on earth, we read, "Through the praise of children and infants you have established a stronghold." That is from Psalm 8:2. There is just something special about children and God and praise.

You'll notice that today I have two rulers. One is taped on the back of this chair, while the other is suspended on the string. Let's say the left side of the hanging ruler is the infants' side, the little babies. On the right are older kids. That would be the children like you. Got it? Infants on the left; children on the right.

Now check this out. I have some clothespins here in my hands. They will represent how much we praise God. We can put different numbers of clothespins on each side of the ruler and always have it balance out. It's true. And we can figure out ahead of time how to balance the clothespins. Watch this. I'll hook two clothespins on the infant's side (two clothespins at two inches). See, two pins at two inches. Two times two is four. Wow, that side really goes down. The infants sure are praising God.

For the other side I only have one clothespin. If I can get it to equal a total of four, the children will balance out the infants. How many inches away would one clothespin have to be so that it has a total downward pull of four? That's right. Four inches. Let's clip it there and see what happens. Yes, perfect! Good call.

Uh-oh, now the infants have three clothespins at four inches. *(Do this.)* They are really trying to get God to lean down and hear their praises. Let's see, three times four gives us twelve. That's a lot of praise. Over here on the children's side I only have two clothespins. Where would I need to put these two clothespins to balance out the infants' side? Great answer—at the six. That's way out on the end. Let's check it out. And, you're exactly right. Both sides, infants and children, are praising God. And that's a good thing. Before you know it, you'll get us grown-ups praising God too. That's a really good thing.

This is one of those experiments you can try at home, kids. While you're doing it, don't forget the whole point. Keep on praising God.

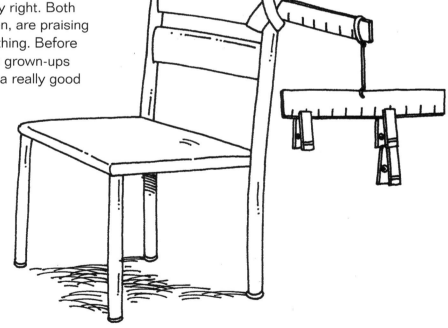

From Mars to the Stars

Psalm 8:3, 4
When I consider your heavens, the work of your fingers, the moon and the stars, which you have set in place, what is mankind that you are mindful of them, human beings that you care for them?

What's Gonna Happen
You're going to inflate a balloon. Can you handle it?

The How Behind the Wow
The big wow in this demo is not the balloon, but the concept. As proposed by Edwin Hubble, our universe is expanding. All the galaxies are moving outward away from each other. This is appropriately known as the expanding universe theory.

What You Need
Balloon (black, if possible)   Wite-Out® correction fluid
Permanent marker   Spring-loaded clothespin

What You Do
1. Inflate the balloon. Twist but don't tie. Use the clothespin to keep it closed.
2. While the balloon is inflated, use either the correction fluid or the marker to draw 30–40 small galaxies at random on the balloon. Correction fluid on a blue or black 12″ balloon is perfect. The galaxies may be just dots on the balloon, or you can try the ideas in the next paragraph.
   Galaxies are giant star islands in space. Stars make up galaxies. Galaxies have three basic shapes. Many galaxies are spiral shaped, like pinwheels. That's the case with our own Milky Way galaxy. A second shape is elliptical, like a starry football. Still other galaxies are irregular, in that they have no particular shape, somewhat like star-filled amoebas.
3. Once the correction fluid or marker has dried, let the air out of the balloon. You'll use this balloon in your talk.
4. Have a great time with this talk. When it comes to science, it doesn't get much more spectacular than astronomy.

What You Say

As you know, our talks lately have been from the book of Psalms. David, who wrote many of the psalms, was a shepherd boy. In those days shepherds weren't out just a little at night, but a lot. David spent many hours looking up at the nighttime sky. He put what he saw, and what he felt, into the words we call *psalms*. Listen to what he says in Psalm 8:3,4: "When I consider your heavens, the work of your fingers, the moon and the stars, which you have set in place, what is mankind that you are mindful of them, human beings that you care for them?"

David knew what it was like to feel small in a vast universe. Maybe you know the feeling. And do you know what? As big as the universe is, it's getting even larger. It's true. Astronomers talk about an expanding universe. Here, I'll show you what I mean with this balloon. As you can see, I've marked on it a bit. Now watch what happens when I inflate the balloon. *(Do this. Pause halfway along.)*

What I've drawn on the balloon are galaxies. Galaxies are made of stars. If you keep your eye on a couple of those galaxies, you'll see them move farther apart as I keep inflating the balloon. *(Blow the balloon larger. Stop when about maxed out. You don't want an exploding universe!)*

See how the galaxies have moved apart? That's like our expanding universe. Will it ever stop? Astronomers think so. What then? Stay put, or start pulling back inward? Wow, lot to think about, huh? But not to worry about, for we're talking a long time from now. If David had known all this back in his day, he would have been even more amazed when he considered the heavens, the work of God's fingers, the moon and stars which God has set in place.

And the same is true for us today. Some night, step outside with your parents, look up at God's Heaven, say a little prayer of thanks, and enjoy the show.

Blue Who?

Psalm 8:6-8

You made them rulers over the works of your hands; you put everything under their feet: all flocks and herds, and the animals of the wild, the birds in the sky, and the fish in the sea, all that swim the paths of the seas.

What's Gonna Happen

You are going to use water of two different temperatures to make the paths of the seas.

The How Behind the Wow

Heat can transfer in three ways. In fluids (liquids and gases) heat transfers by convection currents. Cold fluids condense and sink. Hot fluids expand and rise. As warm substances expand, cold (air or liquid) pushes in beneath. This helps create the lift of the warmer substances. A cycle or current of warm and cold fluids is created. Wikipedia® has a good article on ocean currents.

What You Need

Blue food coloring   Small plastic tub, as see-through as possible
Ice-cube tray   Warm water
Thermos or cooler   Ice
Spoon or plastic glass

What You Do

1. This is not a spur-of-the-moment demo. First, empty an ice-cube tray. Put 12–15 drops of blue food coloring in each of six molds.
2. Fill the six molds the rest of the way with water. Put the ice cube tray in the freezer and allow to freeze.
3. Fill the plastic tub most of the way with warm tap water. Set the tub on a table.
4. Place a blue ice cube in the water at one end of the plastic tub. Cold blue water from the ice cube will stream down to the bottom of the tub, then across to the warmer end. You can follow the stream of cold blue water down from the cube, as well as the flow of blue water across the tub. A blue layer will form on the bottom of the tub.
5. Empty and clean tub. Have fresh water set up for your talk. You will need to keep the blue ice cubes frozen in a cooler or large thermos containing regular ice, or dry ice, if you really want your blue cubes to be cold. And you'll want warm water in your tub. The extra cubes are for any extra testing you might want to do ahead of time. (Note: You can purchase a block of dry ice at a grocery store. Preferably

buy this the day of your talk; no sooner than the day before. The dry ice will be in a plastic bag. Pick it up by this bag. **Never touch the actual dry ice.** Put the block of dry ice in a paper grocery sack and set it into a cooler. Put the lid on.)

6. The spoon or plastic glass are for getting the cube from the thermos.

What You Say

It's interesting how people knew things in Bible days, long before modern technology. Back in those days they didn't have electricity. Certainly they didn't have radio, TV, radar, satellites, or rocket ships. Yet somehow they had a great awareness of the world around them.

Take, for instance, three verses from Psalm 8. Verses 6–8 say, "You made them rulers over the works of your hands; you put everything under their feet: all flocks and herds, and the animals of the wild, the birds in the sky, and the fish in the sea, all that swim the paths of the seas."

That very last phrase is where we're going today: "All that swim the paths of the sea." Today, we call those paths *currents*. In the oceans of the world there are great currents of water, powered by heat from the sun and the rotation of the earth. These currents are like gigantic rivers of water within the ocean's waters. The currents help transport warm water to the poles and colder water toward the equator. There really are paths in the sea.

I'll show you what I mean. I have warm water in this plastic tub. And in my thermos I happen to have some colored ice cubes. I'll get one of the ice cubes out and put it in the water. Here we go. Watch the ice cube closely. Can you see the cold water streaming downward? Sure, you can. Now watch as it moves across the bottom of the tub. Isn't that cool? Actually, it's pretty cold, but it's cool too.

And so it is, we have ocean currents. Or, as David would say, we have the "paths of the sea." Do you see? They knew about the sea. More importantly, they knew the one who made the sea. Still today the paths of the sea are good enough for you and me.

The Choir Has the Fire

Psalm 9:1, 2
I will give thanks to you, LORD, with all my heart; I will tell of all your wonderful deeds. I will be glad and rejoice in you; I will sing the praises of your name, O Most High.

What's Gonna Happen
You're going to swing a birthday candle around in a circle. It will stay lit.

The How Behind the Wow
You will swing a burning birthday candle in a circle. The candle will be in an open-topped bottle. The bottle will protect the candle from the wind, thus allowing the candle to keep burning.

What You Need
2-liter plastic soda pop bottle
Birthday candle
String
Permanent marker
Nail

Matches
Clay
Ruler
Scissors
Paper towel

What You Do
1. Cut three strings, each two feet long.
2. Use the scissors to cut through the label on the two-liter bottle. While holding the glue areas of the label under running hot water, pull the label off of the bottle.
3. Use the ruler to measure seven inches up from the bottom of the bottle. Mark with the permanent marker.
4. Cut around the bottle with the scissors. You only need the bottom of the bottle, but save the top half. You can use it with the "Wind Tunnel in a Funnel" demo on page 35.
5. Hold nail with folded paper towel and heat the nail with a candle. You now have a hot nail and bottom section of the bottle. Use the hot nail to punch three holes around the top of this section. Space holes evenly.
6. Tie the strings in the holes. Bring the strings together above the bottle and tie the three strings together.
7. Put a small amount of clay in the bottom of the bottle.
8. Stand a new candle up in the clay. Light the candle. The easiest way to light the candle is by turning the bottle upside down.
9. Once the candle is lit, swing the bottle in an easy-going vertical circle out in front of yourself. The candle will stay lit throughout the ride. That's it. Blow out the candle and you'll be ready to roll for real.

What You Say

The word *praise* is one of the main words, and thoughts, in the book of Psalms. There are times it seems that David just can't stop praising God. He praises God for God's faithfulness, for his mighty power, for his love, and as it says in our verses today, "I will give thanks to you, LORD, with all my heart; I will tell of all your wonderful deeds. I will be glad and rejoice in you; I will sing the praises of your name, O Most High." Those verses are found in Psalm 9, verses one and two.

As I read through those verses a couple of times, I saw that David not only praised, he sang praise. That reminds me of a choir singing God's praise in church. Singing praise—that's a good thing. It helps us as Christians, but do you know what else? It keeps the light of faith alive so that others might believe. That's right, the more we praise and thank God, the brighter the flame of faith burns for others to follow.

I'll show you what I mean. I have my little faith candle here. As you can see, it's sitting down in what's left of a two-liter bottle. That bottle is like our praises, surrounding the flame of faith, helping it to stay lit. What I'm going to do is light the candle *(do this)*, then swing it in a circle. Normally, swinging a candle around in a circle is not a good thing. The candle almost instantly goes out. But watch what happens with our candle that's surrounded and protected by our praises. *(And away you go!)*

(After 9 or 10 revolutions, ease into a landing.) Are you getting the picture? Somebody before us, probably lots of somebodies, did their part to keep the flame of faith burning brightly. Now it's our turn to do the same for someone else. So let's be like David and praise God every chance we get. It'll do wonders for us . . . and for the kingdom.

Wind Tunnel in a Funnel

Psalm 10:4
In his pride the wicked man does not seek him;
in all his thoughts there is no room for God.

What's Gonna Happen
You're going to try to blow a ping-pong ball out of a funnel. Not gonna happen.

The How Behind the Wow
This is an example of Bernoulli's principle. Faster-moving air has less pressure. Your fast-flowing breath has less pressure than the still air above the ping-pong ball, so the ball won't blow out of the funnel.

What You Need
Ping-pong ball
Funnel

What You Do
1. Hold the funnel with the large opening facing upward.
2. Place the ping-pong ball into the funnel.
3. Blow through the small end and try to launch the ping-pong ball across the room. Just can't do it.

What You Say

Today's psalm is number 10. It's 18 verses long. In almost every one of those verses David complains to God about the bad guys he (David) sees all around him. In today's verse, Psalm 10:4, David writes, "In his pride the wicked man does not seek him; in all his thoughts there is no room for God."

That's pretty shocking, isn't it? Can you imagine people who have absolutely no room for God in their thoughts? They only think about themselves. They are sure they can do anything they want. They don't need anybody or want anybody's help. On top of that, they make life hard for those around them. As far as they're concerned, they can do it all.

Or can they? I wonder if God says, "We'll see just how much they can do on their own"? What if God showed them this little, bitty, lightweight ping-pong ball and a funnel. *(Turn the funnel up and put in the ping-pong ball.)* All they have to do is blow the ball out of the funnel. Are they tough enough to even do that? Well, let's see.

I'll be tough guy number one. "I can blow that ball all the way across the room." *(Go for it, two or three times.)* "What? That's not right. I thought I was tougher than that."

So bad guy number two steps up and says, "You wimp. I'll show you some hot air." *(Try again, even harder.)* "It's just a ping-pong ball. What's going on?" Which brings up the meanest of all, number three. He huffs and he puffs and *(really go for it)* . . . nothing.

So the point of all this is, before folks start talking about how they're tough enough to take on God, they'd better first of all be tough enough *(hold up ball)* to take on a ping-pong ball and funnel. Remember, kids, everyone needs God. Period.

Having a Ball

Psalm 16:2
I say to the LORD, "You are my Lord; apart from you I have no good thing."

What's Gonna Happen
You will blow a stream of air between two ping-pong balls. They will pull toward the air rather than push apart.

The How Behind the Wow
When air is moving it exerts less pressure on objects that it flows beside. In this case, as you blow air between the two ping-pong balls, the moving air in the middle has less pressure than the still air on the outside of the ping-pong balls. The greater pressure of the still air pushes the ping-pong balls toward each other.

What You Need
2 ping-pong balls
Drinking straw
Scissors

Pencil
Lightweight string or thread
Tape

What You Do
1. Cut two 10-inch pieces of string.
2. Tape one end of each string to a ping-pong ball. Only use small amounts of tape.
3. Tape the other ends of the strings to the pencil. On the pencil, tape the strings 2½ inches apart. This will cause the ping-pong balls to hang about ½–¾ inches apart from each other. Be sure that the two ping-pong balls are hanging the same length down from the pencil.
4. Hold the pencil horizontally in front of you so that the ping-pong balls hang down at about your mouth level.
5. Place the straw in your mouth. In a moment you are going to blow gently between the ping-pong balls. The end of the straw should be about four inches behind the ping-pong balls. As you blow through the straw, the ping-pong balls will swing toward each other.
6. Check it out and see if it works for you. It will take a bit of practice. When you've got all your distances worked out, you're ready.

What You Say

(Start off by showing your demo apparatus.) Good morning, everyone. I've got a little ping-pong ball setup to show you today. As you can see, there's a pencil, two strings, and two ping-pong balls hanging down from the pencil. I also have this straw with me.

So with all of these things, let's figure out what we're going to do with them and what the point will be. Psalm 16:2 says this: "I say to the LORD, 'You are my Lord; apart from you I have no good thing.'" That is surely the truth. Our best times ever will be those we spend with God. When we are apart from him, it's just not the same. We find ourselves wanting to get back.

What I'm going to do now is hold the pencil up close to the top of my head. That will let the ping-pong balls hang close to mouth level. I'll hold them out from me just a bit. Now, I'm going to use this straw to blow air between the ping-pong balls. We'll let one of those balls stand for God and the other one stand for us. Question is: As I blow through the straw, will the ping-pong balls move toward or away from each other? *(Accept all answers.)*

All good answers, but there's only one way to find out for sure. So here we go. Watch closely. *(You're on. After your first go-round . . .)* Did everybody see that? The ping-pong balls came together and bounced off of each other. That's pretty cool. Let's slow them down, steady them up, and try again. *(Do again a second time.)* Hey, same thing. The two ping-pong balls always come together.

Come to think of it, that's just like today's verse. Apart from God we have no good thing. So there we go, making sure we're staying close to God. We never want to be apart from him. Let's do this one last time just to make sure. *(Do again a third time.)* Hey, no doubt. We've proved beyond all doubt that we never want to be apart from God.

May "Eye" Help You?

Psalm 17:8a
Keep me as the apple of your eye.

What's Gonna Happen
You're going to put an apple in a Ziploc bag. The apple will stay fresh for a long time.

The How Behind the Wow
Ziploc is just one brand of storage bags that has introduced a vacuum-type bag. You put what looks like an air pump on the indicated location on the bag. Then, when you begin vacuuming, air is pulled out of the bag rather than being pumped into the bag. Taking the air out of the bag makes it possible to store food for a much longer time without the food spoiling.

What You Need
Apple
Ziploc® Brand Vacuum Freezer System and bags

What You Do
1. Wash and dry the apple.
2. If you've just bought a new box and haven't used one of the vacuum pumps, it's very easy. Open the bag and put the apple inside. Zip the bag tightly shut.
3. Lay the bag flat on a table. The vacuum circle should be facing upward.
4. Stand the pump up on the vacuum circle and begin pumping air out of the bag. Fifteen pumps will normally make a good vacuum.
5. Unzip the bag, take out the apple, and have all things ready for your presentation.

What You Say

You may have heard the expression, "The apple of my eye." The phrase appears several times in the Bible, with the earliest being in the book of Deuteronomy 32:10. In the book of Psalms, the expression is found in Psalm 17:8: "Keep me as the apple of your eye." *(Show the apple.)*

When someone or something is the apple of our eye, that means we *really* like it. Do you have anything or anyone who is the apple of your eye? *(Accept all answers.)* Did you know God has someone who is the apple of his eye? It's true and it's not one someone, but a lot of someones. It's us. We all are his creation, so we are the apple of his eye. Pretty cool, don't you think? I do.

One of the words that kind of gets lost in all of this apple doings is the word *keep*. Psalm 17:8 says, "Keep me as the apple of your eye." We are not only the apple of God's eye, he *keeps* us there forever. Doesn't get any better than that, my friends.

All of which brings to mind this storage bag. *(Show.)* This isn't just a zip and shut bag. No way, this is a vacuum bag. See this vacuum pump? *(Show.)* When we use it, we don't pump air into the bag. We pump air out. If there's no air around the food, the food stays fresh way longer. We could say it keeps better.

I'll begin by putting our apple in the bag. *(Do this.)* Now I'll zip the bag shut. Okay, check this out. The vacuum pump goes on this circle, 'cause there's an opening there. Everything is set. Would one of you like to do the pumping? Excellent. Away you go then.

(As air leaves the bag . . .) Hey, look everybody. See how the bag is shrinking around the apple? That's because air is being pumped out. *(When the volunteer has finished . . .)* And we're done. That apple will keep just like it is for a long, long time. Especially if we put it in the fridge. But do you know what? No matter how long this apple keeps, it won't keep nearly as long as you will be kept as the apple of God's eye. And that, my friends, is something to get pumped up about.

You may want to experiment with an apple that has been cut up.

Wind-Wind Situation

Psalm 18:10b
He soared on the wings of the wind.

What's Gonna Happen
You're going to use a leaf blower to blow a roll of toilet paper from here to kingdom come.

The How Behind the Wow
The roll of toilet paper will be on a dowel rod or PVC pipe. You will actually blow just over the top of the roll. Bernoulli's principle says the faster a fluid (gas or liquid) flows, the less pressure it exerts on things it bypasses. This less pressure going over the top of the toilet paper roll causes the paper to unwind and lift into the air.

What You Need
2 rolls of toilet paper
Dowel rod or PVC pipe (no larger than 1" diameter)
Leaf blower
Extension cord
3-prong adapter (optional)
Hacksaw

What You Do
1. Be sure that you unroll the toilet paper a few turns so that it is unstuck from itself.
2. The dowel rod or PVC pipe only needs to be 18" long. Use the hacksaw if necessary.
3. To practice, put the toilet paper roll on the dowel rod. Plug in the extension cord to both the wall and the leaf blower. Have two people hold the dowel rod for you, one on either end. Position the leaf blower just behind and above the top of the toilet paper roll. Fire that thing up and let the horses run. It will make a lot of noise and a bit of a mess, but it's all good. The toilet paper will pick up easily.
4. Plan on having a fresh toilet paper roll for your talk. Again, unwind the roll two or three turns to be sure the paper isn't stuck to itself. Also, check to see if you'll need a three-prong adapter for the extension cord. If so, be sure to take one with you. Roll on.

What You Say

(Leaf blower is out of sight at the beginning.) The word *wind* pops up in the book of Psalms 15 times. Those verses talk about God riding on the wind and things like that. Sometimes you almost get the idea that God and wind go hand in hand. Take Psalm 18:10, for example. That verse says, "He soared on the wings of the wind."

Today, then, we're going to make the wind blow through the trees. Would some of you like to be trees? Great. *(Have the "trees" stand directly in front of the future location of your demo.)* What I need you to do is stand and hold your arms out. Bend them up at the elbows to make tree limbs. Super! You're making great trees.

Wind is moving air. Scientists say that we can't see air and we can't see wind. What we can see is the effect that wind has on things. We can see flags flap in the breeze, leaves blow across the ground, and clouds skim through the sky. So we've got to have something to tell that our wind is actually blowing. And here it is—a roll of toilet paper. I need a couple of you to volunteer to help hold our wind visualizer here. *(Set volunteers up with the toilet paper roll on the dowel rod. Stand behind the roll, facing the "trees.")*

Everything's in place. If we just had some wind, all would be good. Wait, I think I've got it. *(Pull out leaf blower.)* We have wind coming. Okay, everybody ready? Holders? Trees? Watchers? Good deal. Here we go! *(Turn on leaf blower and blow the toilet paper.)*

(At the conclusion . . .) And so, when we see the wind blowing outside, along with watching the flags flap, the leaves loop, and the clouds curl, let's think about Psalm 18:10, God "soared on the wings of the wind."

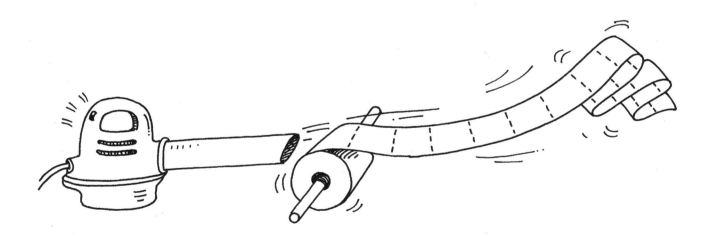

Static in the Attic

Psalm 18:12
Out of the brightness of his presence clouds advanced, with hailstones and bolts of lightning.

What's Gonna Happen
You are going to use static electricity to bend a flow of water.

The How Behind the Wow
Hydrogen and oxygen atoms share electrons to chemically bond into water. This sharing is termed covalent bonding. But the H and O don't share equally. Oxygen pulls the negative electrons a little tighter than the hydrogen atoms do. This makes water a polar covalent molecule. Thus, it has a little positive-negative thing going on. In this demo, the hydrogen in water is attracted by the buildup of electrons on the balloon when the balloon is rubbed with a cloth.

What You Need
Empty soda pop can
Water
Balloons
Plastic tub
Hammer

Nail
Duct tape
Cloth (wool, if possible)
Paper towels

What You Do
1. Use the hammer and nail to make a hole in the bottom of the empty soda can.
2. Put a small strip of duct tape over the hole.
3. Fill the can with water.
4. Put several paper towels in the bottom of the plastic tub.
5. Inflate and tie off the balloon. The tighter the balloon is inflated (within reason), the better.
6. Rub the balloon with the cloth to static up the balloon. Set the balloon aside for the moment.
7. In one hand, hold the can a yard or so above the plastic tub. With your other hand, remove the duct tape.
8. As water falls downward, pick up the charged balloon and hold it near—but not touching—the stream of water. The water will noticeably bend toward the balloon.
9. That's the setup. It's always good to use a fresh balloon at the time of your presentation.

What You Say

The subject today is lightning, those giant streaks of electricity in the sky. Nobody wants to be outside in a storm that has nearby lightning. Especially when those old thunder boomers come along behind.

People knew about lightning back in Bible days. Psalm 18:12 says, "Out of the brightness of his presence clouds advanced, with hailstones and bolts of lightning." When David looked up at those thunderstorms in the sky, with their swirling clouds and great lightning bolts, it reminded him of the very presence of God. Isn't that neat? We can see the hand of God in everything from a flower to a bolt of lightning.

So what exactly is lightning? Anybody know? *(Encourage answers.)* Good answers. Lightning is static electricity. It's not like the electricity in our walls, just waiting to flow to our lights. No, the electricity builds up and builds up, till *ka-zoom,* it jumps across the sky in a gigantic streak that we call lightning.

In honor of lightning we're going to do a little static electricity thing today. I have this inflated balloon and this can of water. The can has a hole in the bottom. That's why the duct tape is there. In a minute we'll take off the tape and let the water run out.

First, though, I'm going to rub my balloon good with this cloth. *(Do this.)* That's building up static electricity. At least, we hope it is. The only way to know for sure is to test it. If one of you will pull off the duct tape, we'll test for static. *(As the duct tape is pulled off, hold the balloon near—but not touching—the falling water.)* Everybody, watch the water closely.

Hey, there's our test. See the water bend? It was attracted to the static electricity on the balloon. You could say we created some static in the attic, just like the lightning back in David's day. And with that we have another reminder of God in our world.

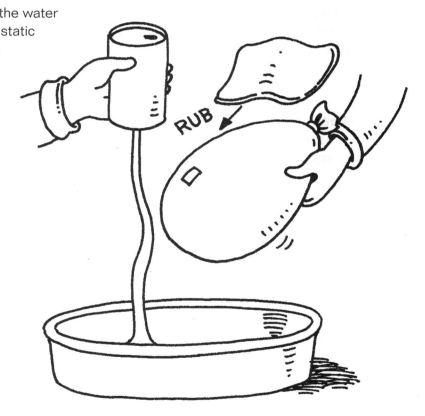

RUB

Star-Spangled Angle

Psalm 19:1a
The heavens declare the glory of God.

What's Gonna Happen
You're going to make an instrument for measuring the angular height of objects in space. It's easy and fun to make. The instrument was first called an astrolabe; later, a sextant. The degrees on your protractor will be the degrees of height of your objects above the horizon.

The How Behind the Wow
Your instrument has only four parts—protractor, straw, string, and weight. Five, if you count tape. The deal here is that the hanging weight is going to respond to gravity, no matter what. As the protractor is swiveled upward, the weight stays put. This allows any angle to be read on the protractor.

What You Need
Protractor

Tape

Scissors

Chair

String

Straw

Weight (e.g., small stone)

Copy of pictures from this demo

What You Do
1. Tape the straw along the straight edge of the protractor but do not cover up the small hole. Cut off any part of the straw that extends past the protractor.
2. Cut a 10-inch piece of string.
3. Tie or tape (or both) the weight onto one end of the string.
4. Tie the other end of the string in the small hole of the protractor. This hole will be just below your straw.
5. Hold your protractor level so that the straight edge is at the top. Notice when the weight is hanging straight down that the reading is 90°, not zero. For this reason subtract your readings from 90°.
6. Put a small piece of tape high on your wall or on the ceiling. Sit in a chair. Look through the straw as you swivel the protractor upwards toward the tape. When you see the tape through the straw, pinch the string against the protractor. This will give you the angle of the tape above the horizon. If it reads 30°, subtract that from 90° and your piece of tape is 60° "high in the sky."
7. Make a copy of the moon, star, sun, and planet patterns. Use the scissors to cut out the copies. Plan on taping these at random heights to the wall and ceiling of your program location. You will have volunteers find the angle height of each of these objects.

What You Say

Have you ever read something in a book that brought a picture to your mind? *(You can let them run with this or not, depending on your time.)* I read a verse in the book of Psalms that painted a picture for me. It's Psalm 19:1 and it says, "The heavens declare the glory of God." Sometimes, whether day or night, looking at the beauty of the sky sure reminds us of the glory of our heavenly Father, doesn't it? He's an amazing creator.

Thinking about that, I made an instrument for locating the height of some of those objects in the sky. *(Show protractor.)* What do you think? It's a protractor, a straw, and a weight on a string. That's all, but it works. Look around you at the wall and ceiling. We have the sun, moon, a star, and a planet taped at various heights. What's really neat is that you—not me, but you—can look through my invention here and find the heights of those objects in the sky. Would some of you like to try it?

(With first volunteer in chair . . .) Okay, look through the straw till you find the star. Let me know when you see it. *(When the star is found, push the string against the protractor to get the reading. Or just look where the string is hanging and subtract the number from 90°. Notice that on the protractor you don't want to use the numbers above 90°. Move through the remaining space objects with other volunteers.)*

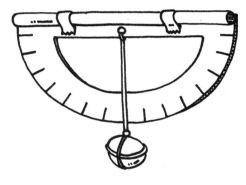

And so, we found all of those objects in the heavens, didn't we? Each of them has a different appearance and is at a different angle in the sky. But all of them are reminders of Psalm 19:1. Do you remember the verse? "The heavens declare the glory of God." Let's never forget his glory when we look—day or night—into the heavens.

Whack-a-Stack

Psalm 23:1
The LORD is my shepherd, I lack nothing.

What's Gonna Happen
You'll make two stacks of nickels, then whack the stacks down with a spatula.

The How Behind the Wow
The mass of each nickel gives it inertia. Inertia is a resistance to change in motion. As you whack nickels from the bottom of each stack, the rest of the stack remains in place.

What You Need
9 nickels
Flat baking pan (optional)
Flat spatula

What You Do
1. This demo definitely takes some practice.
2. Stack the nickels in two stacks (one stack of five; one of four) on a table or counter top.
3. Place the spatula on the counter top. The blade part should be near the stack of nickels. When you flick the spatula sideways, this flat edge will strike the bottom nickel. This will make the bottom nickel zing out, leaving the rest of the stack standing upright.
4. Each time you whack a nickel from stack one, you will say a word from Psalm 23:1, phrase 1: *whack* The . . . *whack* Lord . . . *whack* is . . . *whack* my . . . *whack* . . . shepherd.
5. Each time you whack a nickel from stack two, you'll say a word from Psalm 23:1, phrase 2: *whack* I . . . *whack* lack . . . *whack* nothing . . . *whack* period.
6. Think ahead to the table you will be using. You may have to take a flat baking pan and turn it upside down for a surface.

What You Say

Psalm 119:11 says we are to hide God's Word in our heart. We hide God's Word in our heart by memorizing Scripture. That way the Word is hidden in our heart. Bible memory is a really good thing.

Today we're going to memorize a verse. It's one of the best known in the whole Bible, so you may already know it. The verse is Psalm 23:1. It says, "The LORD is my shepherd, I lack nothing." You've heard that before, haven't you? Sure you have. Just about everybody has. Let's say the verse together. *(Do this.)*

Having the Lord as our shepherd is so huge. Like the verse says, it keeps us from wanting lots of other things. When the Lord is *not* our shepherd, we gotta have this, gotta have that . . . just to try and be happy. But when the Lord is our shepherd, it's a whole new ball game. He is the source of our happiness and joy.

To help memorize this verse, I have two stacks of nickels here. Nine nickels total. I'm going to use this spatula to whack a nickel from the bottom of the first stack. As I whack a nickel, the rest of the stack will remain standing. We hope. What we'll do is say a word from Psalm 23:1 each time I whack the stack. Okay? I want you to help me out here.

Here we go. Let's all say the first five words together, one word per nickel. *(And you're off on phrase one, "The—Lord—is—my—shepherd.")* Great job. Now let's do phrase two, "I lack nothing." Ready? *(Whack the phrase two stack, using the last nickel for the period.)*

There you have it. "The Lord is my shepherd; I lack nothing." Period. Let's always keep God's Word hidden in our heart by memorizing Scripture. He really is our shepherd.

(Optional . . .) Hey, you did such a great job, how about a memory nickel for the road?

Hooping It Up

Psalm 23:3a
He refreshes my soul.

What's Gonna Happen
You'll spin a hula hoop vertically out away from you; it'll come rolling back.

The How Behind the Wow
You're going to throw the hoop forward away from you. At the same time you will be giving the hoop a backward spin. As the spin gains traction on the floor, the hoop first stops its forward travel, then returns back to you.

What You Need
Hula hoop

What You Do
1. The first image of a hula hoop is in the name *Hula.* But the hoop can also be used vertically, which is our goal.
2. Hold the hoop vertically by your side. Throw it away from you. The key to this throw is to give the hoop a sharp, backhanded flick of your wrist. So, even as the hoop travels away from you, it's spinning in a direction that will make it return to you. A little practice and you'll be hooping it up like a pro. In fact, you've probably already done this bunches of times in your younger days.

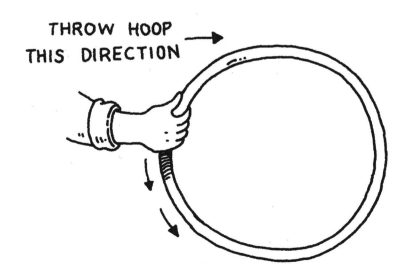

THROW HOOP THIS DIRECTION

What You Say

(Begin with hula hoop out of sight.) The twenty-third psalm is such a classic piece of literature it belongs in a class by itself. David was at the top of his writing skills when he wrote those superb six verses. Each verse is visually and spiritually full of God's grace.

Today we're going to look at one small phrase, just four little words at the beginning of the third verse: "He restores my soul." You see, God is great at many things. At everything, actually. But one thing at which he is especially great is this: restoring our souls. If we ever find ourselves getting even a little bit away from God, he is there to restore our souls. We may forget to give him thanks for his blessings, or we may get upset with someone, or we might get in too big a rush to spend time with him. God is still there to restore our souls. All we have to do is ask.

It reminds me of this *(pull out)* hula hoop. Yes, indeed, a hula hoop. Maybe you've tried keeping one up before. But have you ever tried tossing one out away from you like this? *(Throw hoop out just a bit. Have it come back.)* See how it works? Goes out; comes back. *(Throw it out again, little harder.)* Goes out; comes back. Works every time.

And here's the connection. Sometimes we're like that hula hoop, going out, going out. Keep in mind that we are God's children. He has given us his "God spin." All we have to do is say, "Oops. God, I am so sorry. I want to come back and be tight with you again." And you know what? He *(toss it out yet again, farthest yet. As it comes back to you . . .)* restores our soul.

Bowl and Arrow

Psalm 23:5a
You prepare a table before me in the presence of my enemies.

What's Gonna Happen
You will stand a downward-facing arrow behind a bowl of water. The arrow will then appear to be pointing upward.

The How Behind the Wow
Behind the pupil of our eye is a lens. This lens focuses objects we see onto the retina of the eye. The lens also flips the image of the objects upside down. Our brain then turns this image right side up. With this water bowl demo we are adding yet another lens, which flips things back over again.

What You Need
4 x 6 index card

Water

Ruler

Vegetable can

Marker

Small fish bowl, spherical in shape

Tape

What You Do
1. Place the index card horizontally in front of you. Use the marker and ruler to draw a large arrow from top to bottom on the card.
2. Tape this card to the vegetable can or anything else that will hold the index card straight up. The arrow should be pointing downward.
3. Fill the fishbowl with water.
4. Place the fishbowl on a table. A counter-high table would be best.
5. Stand the can a foot or so behind the bowl.
6. Look through the bowl toward the arrow. It may take a bit for you to work out the best distance. At some point you'll see the arrow. This starts some 2–3 feet in front of the bowl, and stretches out so that you can see the arrow from across the room. Instead of pointing downward, you will see the arrow pointing up.
7. The assumption here is that the kids are somewhat gathered around you as you're giving this talk. If so, you need to plan on either:
    a. having them move to line up with the bowl and arrow, or
    b. leave the children and the bowl as they are, but move the arrow in a semi-circle behind the bowl.

What You Say

One of David's best-known psalms is the 23rd. If you have heard it, then you may recognize this part, "You prepare a table before me in the presence of my enemies." That is Psalm 23:5. Have you heard that before? Uh-huh, I felt sure you had.

Let's take a look at one part of the verse—the enemies. In his day David had enemies. They tried to bring him down. Reminds me of this arrow. *(Show can.)* Can you see which way it's pointing? Sure, you can. Downward. That's what David's enemies did—they tried to bring him down.

Today, you and I do not have the same enemies as David did. But there are voices and choices that would point us away from God. And we don't want that. We want to be pointed up toward God. God wants that too. That's why he prepares a table before us, to help us focus on him.

On the table I'm preparing for you, I'll place an interesting object—a fishbowl with water in it. *(Set up arrow and fishbowl.)* Let's see if that bowl of water can keep all of our attention pointing in the right direction. One at a time I want each of you to look through the bowl at the arrow, okay? *(Help work this out with them.)*

(When finished . . .) Did everybody see the arrow pointing upward? Good, good. The table God prepares for us always does that—points us up toward him.

Falling in Love

Psalm 23:6a
Surely your goodness and love will follow me all the days of my life.

What's Gonna Happen
You will stand two yardsticks up and let them fall sideways. One will always fall faster.

The How Behind the Wow
You will tape equal weights four inches from the end of each yardstick. Stand the yardsticks so that one has the weight at the top; one at the bottom. When you let go of the sticks at the same time, the bottom yardstick always falls faster. Think of the yardsticks not as just falling over, but falling in a circle. The smaller the radius of the circle, the quicker the fall.

What You Need
2 yardsticks
Duct tape
Ruler
16 quarters

What You Do
1. Use the duct tape to tape the quarters together into four small packets of four quarters each.
2. Tape a packet of quarters on both sides of the four-inch mark of one of the yardsticks. Repeat this with the other yardstick.
3. Place the ruler on a table or counter in front of you. The ruler should be pointing straight out away from you. Tape the ruler down.
4. Hold the yardsticks so one of the sticks has the weight at the top, while the other stick has the quarters at the bottom. You are going to stand these sticks partially on the ruler. This gives the sticks a slight sideways tilt. That way when you release them they have to fall toward the down side.
5. Stand the yardsticks so that they are side by side, with one nearer you and one slightly farther away. You should be able to hold them up with one hand. Have your other hand ready to catch them.
6. Let the yardsticks go at the same time. The one with the weight at the *bottom* will fall *faster* than the one with the weight at the top.
7. Repeat this several times to get the feel of the whole setup. You'll always get the same result. For a more dramatic difference between the two falls, add more weight to each yardstick.

What You Say

In the twenty-third psalm there are six verses. Each one stands alone as an important statement to us. Together, the six verses make a powerful message about God and faith.

Have you heard the sixth verse before? It's the one that says, "Surely your goodness and love will follow me all the days of my life." Two good things—goodness and love—are following us all the days of our lives. That is directly because of God. He provides the good things that come with life.

So let's take a look at two good things. I have these two yardsticks with weights taped onto them. I'll stand one of the sticks so that the weight is at the top and stand the other one so the weight is at the bottom. I'll stand them up on the side of this ruler. See how they lean just a bit? That way, when I let them go, they'll fall to that side.

Question is, which one will fall faster—the one with the weight at the top or the one with the weight at the bottom? *(Encourage answers.)* Hey, good answers. Way to think. Now let's find out. Here we go. *(Let sticks fall a foot or so before catching them.)* Did you see which one fell faster? *(They may not have picked up on the faster one.)*

I'll do it again just to make sure. *(Do demo again.)* Same thing. The one with the weight at the bottom falls faster every time. You see, that stick represents goodness. It comes first in the Bible verse. And coming along behind? That would be love. Just like it says in Psalm 23:6, "Surely *(do the demo one last time)* your goodness and love will follow me all the days of my life."

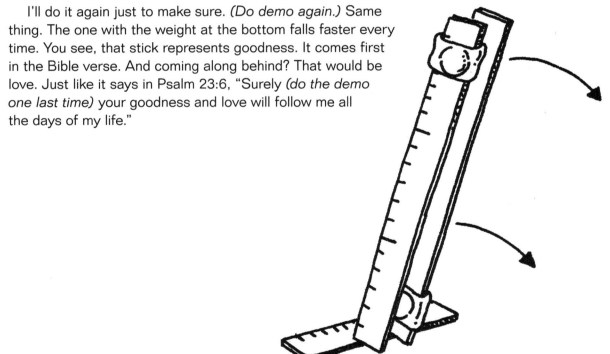

Clean Pure Through

Psalm 24:3, 4a
Who may ascend the mountain of the LORD?
Who may stand in his holy place? The one who
has clean hands and a pure heart.

What's Gonna Happen
You're going to put a bar of Ivory soap in a microwave oven, give it 75 seconds, and
end up with a big pile of soap on your hands.

The How Behind the Wow
As you know, Ivory soap will float. According to Ivory legend, the bar's floating ability
was created when an employee left a stirring machine on too long. The machine
whipped extra air into the soap, lowering its density. Since its density became less
than water, it floated. This mistake stirred up quite a hit. When you microwave your
bar of Ivory, the heat will cause the air inside the soap to expand the melting soap to
several times its original mass. You will end up with a large pile of soap.

What You Need
Microwave oven
2 bars of Ivory soap®
3-prong adapter (optional)

Microwave-safe plate
Extension cord

What You Do
1. Take the wrapper off a bar of Ivory soap. Place the bar on the plate.
2. Set the plate and soap into the microwave oven. Turn the microwave on for 75
    seconds.
3. At the end of the time, take the plate and soap out of the microwave. As the soap
    cools down, it will deflate a bit. However you will still have an impressive, and
    aromatic, mound of soap.
4. Clean up everything and take the second bar with you for your performance. Don't
    forget the microwave, extension cord, and the three-prong adapter.

What You Say

One of the things I like about David is that sometimes he asks a question. Then to make sure we get the right answer, he answers the question. Kind of nice having the answers every now and then.

This is what we have today. In Psalm 24:3 David asks, "Who may ascend the mountain of the LORD? Who may stand in his holy place?" Before we even have time to think about the answer, he gives it to us in the next verse: "The one who has clean hands and a pure heart."

Clean hands and a pure heart. Pretty good company, I'd say. In honor of those two things I have *(show wrapped bar)* a bar of Ivory soap. Hey, it's soap, so there's the clean hands part. Ivory has been around for more than a hundred years. Throughout many of those years, Ivory has been advertised as 99.44% pure. Now that is some pure soap. So right here in my hand I have both those things talked about in Psalm 24:4—clean and pure. Ivory soap is a great reminder of how we're supposed to be before the Lord—having clean hands and a pure heart.

When we are like that, we're proud to be Christians and to have God in our life. Our spirits are enlarged before him. I'll show you what I mean. *(Take off wrapper and microwave soap for 75 seconds. As the microwave is going . . .)* Can you see inside the microwave? Maybe see a little something happening to the soap? I'm thinking so.

(When done, take out the soap.) How about that? Our Ivory soap swelled up right before our eyes. That is just the way our spirits will do when we have clean hands and a pure heart.

Going Green

Psalm 25:4, 5

Show me your ways, LORD, teach me your paths. Guide me in your truth and teach me, for you are God my Savior, and my hope is in you all day long.

What's Gonna Happen

You're going to lower a glass of blue water into a bowl of yellow water, giving you blue, yellow, and green water.

The How Behind the Wow

Two primary colors can blend to give secondary colors. This is especially true with "see-through" colors like food coloring in water. We'll be putting a glass of blue water into a bowl of yellow water. Below the bowl's waterline, the glass will appear to contain green water.

What You Need

Clear glass bowl, like a baking dish
Water
Blue and yellow food coloring
Tall, clear glass or thin vase

What You Do

1. Put 10 drops of blue food coloring in the glass or vase.
2. Fill the glass or vase with water.
3. Put 12 drops of yellow food coloring in the glass bowl.
4. Fill the bowl at least $^2/_3$ full of water.
5. Stand the glass in the bowl. Check to see that the three colors are all easily visible and that there is enough of the green showing below the water line in the bowl. Pour more water into the bowl if you need more green to show.
6. Take the glass from the bowl. Save these things for your talk.

What You Say

Do any of you like to travel? *(Take answers.)* I'm sure you do. Going new places is neat.

Today I have a travel psalm. Let me read it for you. It's Psalm 25:4, 5 and it says, "Show me your ways, LORD, teach me your paths. Guide me in your truth and teach me, for you are God my Savior, and my hope is in you all day long." Do you get it? David was asking for God's guidance as he was traveling his pathway of life. Not a bad thing for us to do either.

And actually, I see these verses in colors. I'll show you what I mean. Here I have a glass of blue water. The blue brings to mind the first part of the verses: "Show me your ways, LORD." Long before there were cars and interstate highways, much of the travel was by ship on the open seas and by boats on the rivers. The ways were blue waterways.

The yellow bowl brings to mind the phrase, "Guide me in your truth." When I think of the truth, I think of being in the light, open and honest before God. And the light is sunny like the yellow of the water in the bowl.

Finally, the last phrase of the verse says, "You are God my Savior." Having a Savior is huge. We all need someone to take us to eternal life someday. When I think of that Savior and eternal life, I think of green. Green valleys are lush with life; deserts on the other hand are not so green, are they? But *(as you look around)* I don't have any green. I ran out of containers, water, and food coloring. I can't show you the green for our Savior unless maybe one of you has an idea. *(Never fear; they'll come through for you.)*

Oh, I get what you're saying. I should set the glass into the bowl. Well, let's check out your idea. Here we go. Hey, you're right. Way to go. You might say, we're "going green." And those are the colors of Psalm 25—blue for God's ways, yellow for the truth, and green for our eternal life with our Savior.

YELLOW   BLUE   APPEARS GREEN

Color My World

Psalm 27:1a
The LORD is my light and my salvation.

What's Gonna Happen
You're going to shine a flashlight onto a CD.

The How Behind the Wow
White light is made of colors. Together the six colors make up the spectrum of white light. These colors are separated by the microscopic ridges of a CD. In some places the waves of color combine with each other to become very vivid; in other places the colors cancel each other out.

What You Need
Flashlight or lamplight
CD

What You Do
1. Shine the light onto the reflective, non-labeled side of the CD.
2. As you move the CD at different angles, you will see both areas of bright colors and areas of no colors. Both areas are termed interference. Positive, or constructive, interference gives the bright areas. Negative, or destructive, interference gives the colorless areas between.
3. In your talk you'll hold the CD facing the children so they can see the colors.

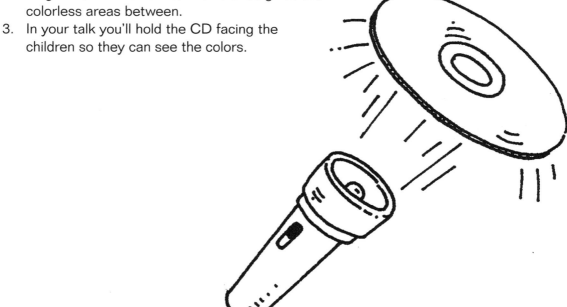

What You Say

(Begin with the CD and flashlight out of sight.) Certain words and ideas carry over straight from the Old Testament to the New Testament. As you know, the book of Psalms is in the Old Testament, which means they were written before Jesus lived on earth. In fact, David, who wrote most of the psalms, was the great-great, umpteenth-great grandfather of Jesus. It says so in the first chapter of Matthew.

But let's get back to words that are found in both parts of the Bible, Old and New. God, for sure. And love. Mercy. And what about light? In Psalm 27:1 David wrote, "The LORD is my light and my salvation." Then, in the New Testament, John began his ministry by stating that Jesus is the light.

Light is a good thing. It brings us visibility, it brings us warmth, it brings us *(show CD)* CDs. What? CDs aren't for light; they're for sound. Yes, they are for sound. But have you ever seen light reflecting off of a CD? Sure, you have. And those colors you see? They remind us that white light is actually made of six colors—red, orange, yellow, green, blue, and purple.

Let's shine our flashlight onto the CD. *(Do so.)* Can you see those colors? Some of you may be seeing red, others yellow, some of you green, others maybe blue. Those are the colors that blend together to make white light. The CD is separating them out from each other. And as I move the CD, the colors change, don't they? Pretty neat.

(With flashlight off, CD facing away . . .) Those colors blending together remind me how the whole Bible—Old Testament and New Testament—blends together to give us a complete picture of God the Father, Son, and Holy Spirit. Those three give us lots of things—especially the spiritual light of truth. May we each walk in that light every day.

Getting in Shape

Psalm 28:8a
The LORD is the strength of his people.

What's Gonna Happen
You're going to make three paper towers, then check them for strength.

The How Behind the Wow
Three pieces of card stock paper become a round column, a triangle one, and a square column. The round column will be the strongest; it has no seams or creases where a weakness would show up.

What You Need

Card stock paper	At least 10 medium-weight books (e.g., hymnals)
Ruler	Small square of plywood or something similar
Pen or pencil	Transparent tape

What You Do
1. Tear 12 pieces of tape and have them ready for use. The pieces should be about two inches long.
2. Have the paper in front of you with the lengthwise direction going from side to side. The 8½ inch direction will stand upright.
3. Column One—**Circle.** Curl the first piece of paper so that there is a 1½ inch overlap. This will be your round column. Tape with four pieces of tape. When done, this column should be three inches in diameter.
4. Column Two—**Triangle.** Place the ruler across the piece of paper. Make dots with your pencil at the following locations: 3¼ inches, 6½ inches, and 9¾ inches. Move your ruler down the paper and make the same marks once again. Draw vertically through the dots with the ruler. Place the ruler on each line and fold. When you finish with each line you'll have a triangle with a 1¼ inch overlap. Tape the column.
5. Column Three—**Square.** Make the square as in step 4, with the following measurements: 2½ inches, 5 inches, 7½ inches, and 10 inches.
6. At this point you have the things for your talk. You can either test these and then make more, or go with what you have. Have 8–10 books and the plywood for a testing base. Congratulations. You are now an engineer for the Lord.

What You Say

I've got some science for you today. Science is all around us, you know. Today we're looking at the science of engineering.

Let's read Psalm 28:8. That verse says, "The LORD is the strength of his people." So we're talking about the science of strength, of building and construction, of holding things up. In other words, engineering.

Look at what I've engineered. Three columns—round, triangle, and square. They're made out of card stock paper. *(You might have a piece of flat card stock to show them.)* It's stronger than regular white paper. Now you and I could just say, "I think the square column is the strongest," and let it go at that. Scientists want to find out for sure though. That's why, along with the columns, I have some testing things: a flat platform base and some books.

Here we go. Let's do the square first, what do you say? *(Place square on board; stack first book flat on top of column.)* By the way, when scientists run tests, they first make a *hypothesis*. That's a statement about the outcome of the experiment. So let's make a hypothesis about these columns. How many say the square will hold the most books? What about the round one? And the triangle? *(You might want to ask adults what they think, as well.)*

Hey, all good hypotheses. So, let's check it out. You count with me as we go. And remember the point of all this—Psalm 28:8—God is our strength. *(Continue adding books to the square column until it collapses, then test the triangle, then finish off with the round column.)*

(When finished, hold up the winning column, round or otherwise.) Just like this column held the most weight, the Lord is our greatest source of strength. So let's stay in shape by always trusting in him.

God Is Good All the Time

Psalm 31:19a
How abundant are the good things that you have stored up for those who fear you.

What's Gonna Happen
You're going to shake a bag of beans and, *voila!* A golf ball will pop up.

The How Behind the Wow
As you shake the dried beans in the plastic bag, the beans settle into spaces. Beans gather under the golf ball, which begins at the bottom of the bag. As you keep shaking the bag, the beans continue settling into gaps and spaces. In the process they force the golf ball up to the surface.

What You Need
Quart-size plastic bag
Golf ball
Bag of dried pinto beans or similar

What You Do
1. Put the golf ball in the plastic bag.
2. Pour in the beans, covering the golf ball and filling the bag halfway. Zip the plastic bag shut.
3. Holding the bag at each end, begin shaking the bag back and forth sideways. Soon the golf ball will rise to the surface. Soon in this case is around 20–30 seconds.
4. Start your actual talk with the golf ball and beans already in the bag. The golf ball will be at the bottom, of course.

What You Say

(Start out by showing the bag of beans.) Today I've got a bag of beans. At the bottom of the bag is a golf ball. What I want to do is get the golf ball to come to the top. Any ideas? Uh-huh, turn the bag over. Could do that. Push up from underneath. Yep, that would work, I imagine. But you know what I'm going to do? I'm going to shake the bag. That's right, just shake the bag. As I do, the beans will settle more and more to the bottom. They'll push upward on the golf ball and before you know it, the golf ball will rise to the top.

This whole process brings to mind Psalm 31:19: "How abundant are the good things that you have stored up for those who fear you." To have fear of God is to have a deep awe of his majesty and power. He has great things stored up for you, your life, your family. The more you are in awe of God the more you will begin to experience the things he has stored up for you.

That golf ball is like the really neat, stored-up goodness of God. Let's see if we can get it to come to the surface, shall we? Good, here we go. *(Shake bag. As golf ball rises to the top . . .)* And so, keep your eyes on the prize of being in awe of God. You will experience the great goodness he has stored up for you.

Hey, that was fast. How about I put the golf ball back on the bottom and let one of you shake the bag? Sound like a good idea? I think so too. Okay, here we go.

Standing for the Lord

Psalm 33:11
But the plans of the LORD stand firm forever, the purposes of his heart through all generations.

What's Gonna Happen
You will stand a foam cup and a plastic glass in a tub of water. The foam cup will remain standing; the plastic glass will fall over every time.

The How Behind the Wow
Styrofoam is an air-filled member of the plastic family. That lighter weight, plus the fact that water doesn't attract to it so much, allows the cup to remain standing. On the other hand, the heavier, slick plastic glass has no chance. It falls every time. (An extension of this is this demo: If you static up a balloon, you can use the balloon to pull the foam cup back and forth across the water. Then you'd have a separate talk about God's guidance.)

What You Need
20 oz. Styrofoam™ cup
Plastic glass
Ruler

Plastic tub (at least shoe box size)
Water

What You Do
1. The cup and glass should be nearly identical in size. Each needs to be at least six inches tall. Check with the ruler. The foam cup I use is a medium Sonic® cup. Everybody has plastic glasses around.
2. Fill the plastic tub ½–¾ full of water.
3. Stand the foam cup in the water. It remains upright.
4. With the foam cup still standing in the water, place the plastic glass on top of the water. It should fall over almost instantly. If it doesn't, use your finger to put just a little water on the outside of the glass. This only has to be on one side of the glass. The plastic glass will fall toward the water side every time.
5. Try to stand the plastic glass some 10 times. Just won't stand.
6. Before your talk you might want to get the plastic glass a little wet as in step 4.

What You Say

In the book of Psalms one excellent verse has to do with the character of God. When we use the word *character*, we're talking about what someone is like. We might use descriptions like, "That guy's a shady character." Or "She has outstanding character." Character is how we are on the inside, in our heart. We always want to have good character.

One verse in Psalms that talks about God's character is Psalm 33:11. It says, "But the plans of the LORD stand firm forever, the purposes of his heart through all generations." Do you see his character in that verse? His plans stand firm forever, the purposes of his heart are the same for all time. That is some amazing character. And he wants us to have the same type of character—steady and true, standing firm.

It reminds me of this tub of water and these two containers. *(Show all.)* One is a slick plastic glass and the other is a foam cup. Almost exactly the same size, aren't they? Let's set them in the water and see if they both stand. Remember our verse: "The plans of the Lord stand firm forever." Standing is a good thing.

We'll start with the foam cup. Hey, it's doing great. Standing like a rock. Now let's try the plastic glass. Oops, that's not good. *(Try again.)* Hmm, fell over again. I'm not so good at this. Do any of you think you can do better? *(Let as many try as your time allows.)* Wow, none of us could get the plastic glass to stand in the water. It fell over every time. But check out the steady foam cup. Still standing.

And that, my friends, is the way God stands steady throughout all generations. He never changes. His character is perfect. Let's you and I always stand on our faith in the Lord. After all *(put in foam cup one last time)*, standing is a *really* good character trait.

What's Up with the Cups?

Psalm 34:3
Glorify the LORD with me; let us exalt his name together.

What's Gonna Happen
You're going to stand on paper cups. They won't flatten out.

The How Behind the Wow
If you stand on one paper cup, the cup has no chance. But 80 cups? The cups rule. It's all about pressure, which is force divided by area. The extra cups provide more area, spreading out the force. This equals success for the cups.

What You Need
2 pieces of ¼" plywood, each 2 feet square (sold already-sized at home improvement stores)
5 oz. paper cups (box of 90)
2 chairs
Oreo® cookies (enough for each child to have one)

What You Do
1. If possible, it would be best to set this up at the presentation site.
2. Place one piece of plywood on the floor. If you have the 2 x 2 foot squares, you can get nine rows of nine cups on the board. Put the cups *upside down* on the bottom board.
3. Place the second piece of plywood on top of the cups.
4. Set the chairs on either side of the plywood, with the backs facing inward toward the plywood. Using the chair backs for support, lower yourself onto the top board. Here's hoping. If you'd rather, you can just wait and let a child be the first.
5. If you have set all this up in your presentation area, you're good to go. Otherwise, you'll need to take apart and reassemble things.
6. Last thoughts: Be sure to have one extra cup with you during your talk. Don't forget the two chairs. Also have the Oreos.

What You Say

(Begin with your cup setup in plain view.) Hello. Today I have a gigantic plywood and paper cup Oreo cookie sandwich. The two pieces of plywood are like the cookie part of the Oreo, while the cups are the filling. All we need is a little milk.

This setup is going to help us remember a great verse. It's Psalm 34:3 and it goes like this: "Glorify the LORD with me; let us exalt his name together." There are some excellent words in that psalm—words like *glorify, Lord, exalt,* and *name.* But one of the words I like best is the very last word—*together.* Kids, when we work together— whether as a family, a team, a class, or a church—good things happen. We're able to do more, learn more, have a better time, and even handle stress better. Teamwork is the best.

I'll show you what I mean about working together. Check this out. Here I have a single paper cup. *(Show cup.)* I'm going to set it upside down on the floor. What do you think will happen if one of you stands on the cup? Will it hold you up, or will you flatten out that cup like a pancake? *(Allow responses.)* Well, let's find out, shall we? Who would like to step on the cup? Good, have at it. Wow, that's even flatter than a pancake.

Now take a look at our plywood-and-paper- cup Oreo. Rather than one cup between those pieces of wood, there are 81 cups. Those cups will spread out the weight of the person. So let's try again. Volunteer, you're on. Use the chair backs to lift yourself up and ease down onto the plywood. Go easy, but have at it. *(Have someone sitting in each chair to make sure the chairs don't tip over.)*

(When success has been achieved . . .) Look, she is standing straight up. No problems. Everything is cool. Life is good. Why is that? *(Allow responses.)* Exactly! The cups worked together to support the weight. All of which brings to mind Psalm 34:3, "Glorify the LORD with me; let us exalt his name together." *(Pull out your Oreo package.)* In honor of our plywood-and-paper-cup Oreo, how about a cookie as you go? And remember, together is a good thing.

Chase the Taste

Psalm 34:8a
Taste and see that the LORD is good.

What's Gonna Happen
You will get a volunteer whose eyes are closed to eat some Starburst candies. He will do this while smelling an onion.

The How Behind the Wow
They ("they" being people who test these things) say that we taste as much with our noses as with the taste buds on our tongues. I'm thinking those "I-can't-taste-anything-because-I-have-a-cold" times support this idea. You will run your own taste test with this demo.

What You Need
Starburst® fruit chews
Onion
Plastic bag

Toothpicks
Knife

What You Do
1. Buy a pack or two (always need pass arounds) of Starburst fruit chews candy. The original flavors are lemon, cherry, strawberry, and orange. Other flavors are also available these days.
2. Eat a couple of pieces of candy, just to see if your taste buds match up with the names on the candy wrappers.
3. Once that's established, cut off a small piece of the onion and kabob it on the end of the toothpick. Hold the onion directly under your nose while you eat another of the candies. Well, what do you think? Can you taste the correct flavor of the candy?
4. That's the demo. For your talk you're going to need two volunteers. Both will have their eyes closed during the taste test. However, only one of them will have the onion below the nose. The other will get to eat the candy straight up. For your time purposes, you can decide on the number of candies they will test.
5. Keep the onion stored in a plastic bag. Have a fresh onion slice on a toothpick for your talk.

What You Say

There's an interesting line in Psalm 34:8. It says, "Taste and see that the LORD is good." You might not think the Lord's goodness would be something we can taste. In a way, though, the more we read the Bible and the more we spend time in church, the more we start saying, "This is great. I love this life." It's so good we can taste it.

Thing is, we don't want anything to come between us and tasting the Lord's goodness. No matter what, let's keep God first in our lives.

I'll show you what I mean. I'm going to need two volunteers today. Great. Both of you are going to close your eyes and taste a piece *(or two or more pieces—your choice)* of Starburst candy. How does that sound? I need one of you to also do a little smell test at the same time. Which one wants to do that? Good deal.

So here we go. Both of you close your eyes. First, I'll unwrap a candy, leave it on the paper, and give it to our "un-smell" volunteer. Okay, volunteer number one, chew it up good. And what flavor do you think it is? That's right! *(We certainly hope.)*

Now for our "smell" volunteer. I'll unwrap your candy and get it ready. But, as you taste, you'll also be smelling an onion. I'll hold that onion just beneath your nose. Isn't that exciting? You're in the middle of a science experiment. *(Do all this.)*

(After a bit . . .) Okay, what do you think the candy flavor was? *(Let's hope they don't have a clue. But if they get it right, you'll think of something. You always do, like maybe, "You got it right, but did the smell take away some of the flavor?")* Sorry, too bad. It was actually _____. Does everybody see what I mean? To fully enjoy being able to experience the Lord's goodness, we need to chase the taste and let nothing else get in the way.

Spectacular Binoculars

Psalm 34:8a
Taste and see that the LORD is good.

What's Gonna Happen
You will have one of the kids help you drop a quarter into a glass. Kind of difficult, actually.

The How Behind the Wow
Our two eyes give us what is called binocular vision. This *really* helps us with depth perception. With one eye closed we lose much of our ability to perceive depth.

What You Need
Glass
Table
Quarter

What You Do
1. Set the glass on a table.
2. You stand on one side of the glass, about six feet away from it.
3. Directly across the glass from you will be your test subject. He should be standing some nine feet back from the glass. It is very important that you, the glass, and the volunteer are in a straight line with each other.
4. Your volunteer closes one eye, while you hold the quarter out at shoulder height and arm's length in front of you. You will slowly move forward toward the volunteer and toward the glass, as well. The volunteer's task is to tell you when to drop the quarter so it lands in the glass.
5. You'll need to explain step 4 to the volunteer. That's the whole deal. It would be a good idea to practice ahead of time with someone.

What You Say

You may recall that we have already talked about today's verse. It is Psalm 34:8 and it says, "Taste and see that the LORD is good." We did a taste test of Starburst candy, and an onion was also involved. *(Only mention this if you've done the "Chase the Taste" demo.)*

Psalm 34:8 has two ways for us to experience God's goodness. It says, "Taste and *see* that the LORD is good." Today, we're going to talk about sight. We have two eyes, right? Here's the thing about having two eyes. Each eye looks at objects from a slightly different angle. That really helps us tell how far away the objects are. One eye? Not so easy.

Not sure we're on to something here? Let's find out then. I need a volunteer. Good. It's always good the way you all step up to help out. So here we go. I'm going to set this glass on the table. You're going to stand over on this side *(show where),* and I'll be over here on this side. See how we're in a straight line? That's a good thing.

In my hand I have a quarter. I'll hold it out like so, then I'll begin to walk toward the glass. Your job is to tell me when to drop the quarter so that it lands in the glass. Easy enough? Sure it is. Just before we start, though, there is one other thing. You have to close one eye. That's the spirit. So here we go. *(I have never had anyone get this on the first go-round. For your sake, I hope your volunteer isn't the first.)*

Oops. Not so close. Sorry. Our two eyes really do help, don't they? And who gave us our two eyes? Right. God. And what does Psalm 34:8 say God wants us to do with those eyes? That's right. He wants us to see how good he is. And God is *very good.*

Wanna try again?

Be Like the One You Like

Psalm 35:10a
My whole being will exclaim, "Who is like you, LORD?"

What's Gonna Happen
You'll turn white carnations blue and red.

The How Behind the Wow
Plants lose water as water vapor passes out through pores called stomates. This process is called transpiration. Transpiration is a really good thing, 'cause it puts a slight pull on water in the roots. This causes water to move upward in plants. The stomates are mostly on the underside of leaves, but sometimes on the petals of plants too. This is the case with the carnations as transpiration pulls the water and food coloring upward to color the petals.

What You Need
3 clear glasses or bud vases
Red and blue food coloring
Scissors

Water
6 white carnation flowers

What You Do
1. Buy six white carnations. Cut the stems so that each stem is some 10–12 inches long. Make the cuts right above the knots on the stems.
2. In one glass, put 12 drops of blue food coloring. Fill half the glass with water. Put two carnations in this glass.
3. In a second glass, put 12 drops of red food coloring. Fill half the glass with water. Put two carnations in this glass.
4. In the third glass, fill half with water. No food coloring. Put two carnations in this glass.
5. You'll be able to see a definite change after one day. If that needs to work in your time frame, you're good to go. Two days will be even better.
6. As you can see, you only need three carnations. The extra one in each glass is just for backup and added effect.
7. Take all glasses, water, and carnations with you for your talk.

What You Say

(Begin with all vases and flowers out of sight.)

Hey, I've got a thought for you today. It's an important thought. See if it works for you. Here it is: we become *like* the things we *like*. Did you get that? The things we like become part of our life. They shape and color the way we think and act. That can be a really good thing when we spend our time in the presence of God.

Today's verse from the book of Psalms will show you what I mean. The verse is Psalm 35:10 and it goes like this: "My whole being will exclaim, 'Who is like you, LORD?'" On one hand the answer to that question is . . . nobody. No one has the power, love, patience, and care that God does. On the other hand we can answer that question by trying our best to be like God.

I'll show you what I mean. *(Show white carnations in clear water.)* Here I have two white carnations. They're pretty flowers, don't you think? I do. You sure see a lot of them in floral arrangements, bouquets, and things like that.

Check this out. At the same time that I put these two carnations in clear water, I put two other carnations in water with blue food coloring. *(Show these.)* How about that? The flowers pulled the blue food coloring up to the petals, turning them blue. Pretty, don't you think? Me too. And that's what I'm trying to say about being like God. The more we're around him, the more we will learn his ways and his will. Those things will color our world and life, making us more like our heavenly Father every day.

With that in mind, what color do you think the carnations are that I put in red water? I'm thinking you are so exactly right. Let's find out, shall we? *(Show glass with red water and flowers.)* Sure enough, you've got it. And you will always have it, my friends, if you spend your days absorbing all you can of God's love and his Spirit.

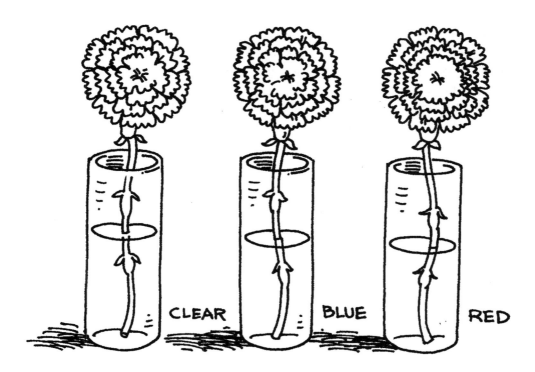

CLEAR   BLUE   RED

As High as the Sky

Psalm 36:5
Your love, LORD, reaches to the heavens, your faithfulness to the skies.

What's Gonna Happen
You're going to balance a yardstick . . . way up.

The How Behind the Wow
It's easier for us to balance taller objects than shorter ones. Visualize things not just falling over, but falling in a circle. The larger the radius of the circle, the slower the fall. Therefore, it's easier to balance a yardstick than a ruler on our fingers. A little weight at the top helps both sticks.

What You Need
Ruler
Markers
Duct tape
12 quarters

Yardstick
Scissors
Piece of card stock paper (plain paper will work)

What You Do
1. Draw, color, and cut out a nice-size heart on the paper.
2. Roll a small piece of duct tape so the sticky side is facing out. Put this on the back center of the heart.
3. Tear or cut off six inches of duct tape. Tear this lengthwise into three strips. Tape one of the strips around three of the quarters, making them into a small package. Tape another strip around three more quarters. Use the third strip to tape these two quarter packs to one end of the ruler (three quarters go on each side of the ruler). This now becomes the top of the ruler.
4. Repeat step 3 with the other six quarters, but tape them to the top of the yardstick.
5. Stick the heart to the quarter pack on the ruler, with the bottom of the heart pointing down the length of the ruler. At the opposite end, balance the ruler on your finger. It can be done, but it's not too stable.
6. Do step 5 with the yardstick. Transfer the heart from the ruler to the yardstick.
7. You're ready. Kids are natural balancers. They would love doing this one, if time and circumstances allow.

What You Say

Here's a neat verse for today. It's Psalm 36:5, "Your love, LORD, reaches to the heavens, your faithfulness to the skies." Don't you like that? God's love reaches up to the heavens and his faithfulness to the skies. That's a lot of upward stretch. Only God could reach that high.

But you know what? We can reach a little ways like that. I'll show you what I mean. Here I have a heart. *(Show the heart.)* The psalm talks about God's love, so this heart stands for God's love. And remember, it reaches to the heavens. So somehow I've got to figure out a way to balance it up high. Maybe this ruler will work. What do you think? I'll just tape the heart to these quarters at the top and we'll find out. *(And away you go.)*

(After two or three tries . . .) Whoa, that's not too steady. Maybe the problem is that I didn't have the heart lifted up high enough. After all, the verse says that God's love reaches all the way to the heavens. Think what I'll do is go for something even higher, like this yardstick. Do you think that will be easier or harder to balance than the ruler? *(Allow responses.)* All good answers. Let's find out. I'll take the heart off of the ruler and put it on the yardstick and here we go.

(After a minute of huge success . . .) The yardstick worked much better because it lifted God's heart even higher. In the same way, the higher we lift God's heart in our lives, the better everything will go for us too. So would one of you like to try it?

Mountains of Fountains

Psalm 36:9
For with you is the fountain of life; in your light we see light.

What's Gonna Happen
You'll drop four Mentos chewy mints into a two-liter of Diet Coke and . . . instant fountain!

The How Behind the Wow
According to Mythbusters, a science entertainment TV program, the reaction occurs because of:

a. the combination of ingredients in the two substances, and
b. the surface of the Mentos mints. There are microscopic pits on the surface of the mints. Carbon dioxide gas bubbles in the soda gather in these indentions. The CO_2 gas then releases—very quickly.

What You Need
Large plastic tub, small plastic pool, plastic drop cloth, trash bags, or combo
2–2-liters Diet Coke® or diet root beer
Mentos® chewy mints (Blue pack = super eruption; fruit pack = mild eruption. Be sure that you get mints, not gum. The mints will be in a paper wrapper.)
Cloth towels

What You Do
1. First, and most importantly, go outside. Set the two-liter on the ground. Don't put the two-liters in the fridge beforehand.
2. Take three or four mints out of the blue pack (white Mentos mints).
3. Open the 2-liter. Curl your fingers so that your hand is a vertical tube. Hold the mints loosely in your "hand tube." Drop all of the mints in at the same time. Step back quickly. You only get one shot per two-liter.
4. Save this as an outdoor demo, or figure out the best way to do this indoors without making a huge mess. You'll need a tub or pool, drop cloth or trash bags, maybe a towel or two. It's worth the trouble.
5. If you need any additional ideas, just do an Internet search for "Mentos and Diet Coke."

What You Say

Do you like fountains? Maybe you've made one with a hose in the summertime—either a spray fountain, a gurgly fountain, or a run-it-over-my-head fountain. Fountains are cool. The city of Rome in Italy has the most fountains of any city in the world. In the United States, Kansas City, Missouri, is the City of Fountains.

The most important fountain, however, is found in the book of Psalms. Psalm 36:9 says, "With [God] is the fountain of life." Having water bubbling up is soothing and relaxing. Having God's Spirit bubbling up within us is not only soothing, it's energizing and exciting. Everybody in the world needs God's fountain of eternal life.

So in honor of fountains, today I have a Diet Coke and some Mentos mints. We'll do this demo in this tub (or pool) because fountains have been known to get carried away with themselves. I'll just put the bottle in the middle and undo the cap. Now let's get a few of the mints out. Okay, here we go. Are you ready to see a fountain? Don't be too close, because *(let 'em fall)* we have a mountain of a fountain!

Like they say on TV, don't try this at home, kids. Or, if you do, at least make sure your parents know what's going on and do it outdoors. As for the fountain of God's love—hey, you can try that anywhere.

The Air up There

Psalm 37:4
Take delight in the LORD, and he will give you the desires of your heart.

What's Gonna Happen
You're going to make a little cruising hovercraft.

The How Behind the Wow
The balloon will blow air downward through the CD. The air will hit the tabletop. According to Newton's third law of motion, "every action has an equal but opposite reaction." The air pushing downward against the table will cause the hovercraft to lift just a bit from the table and ride on air.

What You Need
Old CD

9" balloons

Paper towel

Hot glue gun and sticks

2-liter bottle cap

Nail (medium to large)

Heat source (Sterno® or candle)

What You Do
1. Plug in the hot glue gun.
2. Heat the nail over the candle or Sterno. While heating and using the nail, hold the nail with a folded paper towel.
3. Use the hot nail to punch a hole through the bottle cap. Do this from inside out on the cap.
4. Have the CD facing so that the music side is down and the label is facing up toward you. Use the hot glue gun to glue the bottle cap onto the top center of the CD, covering the hole.
5. Press down on the bottle cap while the hot glue is drying.
6. Inflate a balloon. For this demo a 9" balloon is perfect (7" is too small; 12" is too large). Twist closed, but don't tie the balloon. Stretch the balloon mouth over the bottle cap. Set the hovercraft on a table. The slicker the table, the better. Untwist the balloon, and awayyy we goooo.
7. There you are. Go forth and glide. Have an extra balloon, in case.

What You Say

Psalm 37:4 has an amazing promise. That verse says, "Take delight in the LORD, and he will give you the desires of your heart." When we begin delighting ourselves in the Lord, something very interesting begins to happen. The desire of our heart is to keep on delighting ourselves in him—wanting to be in his presence, having fellowship with him, just enjoying our relationship. Our days go smoother as we delight ourselves in the Lord.

Tell you what, delighting ourselves in the Lord reminds me of this CD. *(Hold up CD without balloon; underside toward the kids so they can't see the bottle cap.)* This is an old CD, got scratches on it, probably couldn't even play music anymore. But you know what it can do? It can show us something about riding through each day with God.

Check this out. *(Show bottle cap.)* See, I put a nail hole through this bottle cap. Then I hot-glued the bottle cap onto the CD. What I've made is a hovercraft, a structure that rides on air. All I need is a little source of air. I just happen to have . . . ta-da . . . a balloon! So here I go, blowing up the balloon. *(Do this.)* Now I'll twist it on the cap, set my hovercraft on this table, let the balloon untwist, and . . . Wow, look at that CD. It never had so much fun. Back in its good days it just went round and round in a circle. Now, however, it is going somewhere as it glides on air.

And that is us, kids, when we are delighting ourselves in the Lord. We are going somewhere for the kingdom. Why, some days it even feels as if we're riding on air.

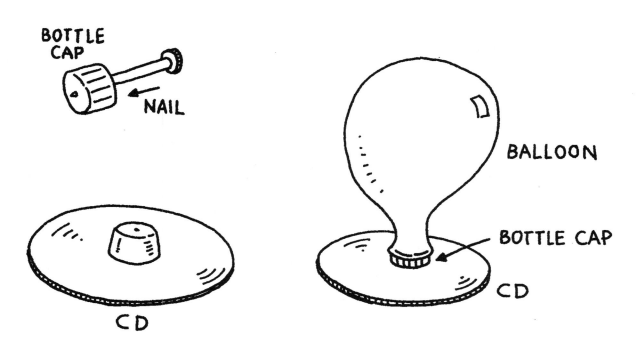

Steppin' Out

Psalm 37:23
The LORD makes firm the steps of the one who delights in him.

What's Gonna Happen
You're going to make some steps out of books, then walk a Slinky down those steps.

The How Behind the Wow
Have you ever tried sending a Slinky down a flight of stairs, and it didn't work? If so, it wasn't you and it wasn't the Slinky. It was the stairs. If stairs are wide enough for walking, they are too wide for a Slinky. So the steps you build will be about half the normal width of stairs. And, like that, your Slinky will be good to go!

What You Need
Set of large books, such as encyclopedias
Slinky® (metal)
Facial tissue box (unopened)

What You Do
1. Buying a Slinky isn't as easy as it once was. If Walmart doesn't have them, you need to try either a variety-type store or go online. Only use a plastic Slinky as a last resort.
2. On the table, use the encyclopedias to build a flight of stairs. One possible arrangement of books is shown for your reference, but other designs will also work. The main thing is you want the steps to be some 5 inches high and 5½ inches wide.
3. The top step is the unopened facial tissue box.
4. Set your Slinky on the top step (tissue box). Give it a looping pull toward the next step and let it go. It should "walk" all the way down to the table. Of course, *should* and actually *doing* are two different things. So practice a few times. You'll find that the main thing is hitting the right location on the first step downward.
5. When things go just right, the Slinky will do an extra flip on the table.
6. You're good to go. If you are practicing in a place other than your presentation area, set up your steps in the real deal place.
7. By the way, the tissue box top step can be vertical for added effect.

What You Say

(Hold up Slinky.) Hey, have any of you ever seen one of these? No doubt. It's a Slinky, a world-class toy. You can sling it back and forth in your hands *(do this),* or you can sling it by one hand and let part of it drop till it boings back up. Slinkys are a ton of fun. The best thing they can do, though, is walk down steps. Just like these steps I have here.

Seeing these steps and this Slinky reminds me of a Bible verse. It is Psalm 37:23 and it says, "The LORD makes firm the steps of the one who delights in him." If the Lord delights in all of our ways, he makes our steps firm. God is with us, firming up our spiritual steps.

If you've ever tried a Slinky going down the stairs and it didn't work, the problem wasn't you or the Slinky. The problem was the width of the stair steps. Most stairs are too wide for a Slinky. But not our book and tissue box stairs. They are just right. See, I'll show you. Are you ready? *(Okay, you're on.)* How about that? All the way to the bottom. It even made an extra step on the table. That Slinky is good to go.

In the same way, boys and girls, you and I will always be good to go if we allow God to make our spiritual steps firm in him. All we need to do is delight in him. And making God happy is always a good thing for us to do.

Hey, you want to see the Slinky go down the steps again? Better yet, would one of you like to try it? Okay, here you go. Let's make those steps firm in the Lord.

Weight for the Lord

Psalm 37:34a
Wait on the LORD, and keep his way *(KJV)*.

What's Gonna Happen
You will hang a plastic bag off of a yardstick. In the bag will be a Bible.

The How Behind the Wow
The two main forces at work on structures are tension and compression. When you hold the yardstick flat there is a lot of tension on the stick because the weight pulls the stick over in an arch. When the yardstick is held on edge, though, there isn't near the bend in the stick. The compressional forces that are within the stick balance the downward tension created by the weight.

What You Need
Yardstick
Plastic bag with handles from a grocery or other store
Small Bible

What You Do
1. Hold the yardstick at one end. The stick should be flat horizontally.
2. Put the Bible in the plastic bag. Tie the bag over the end away from your hand.
3. When you let the bag hang on its own, the weight of the Bible will pull the stick far over. In fact, you'll have to make sure you don't use too large a book or too lightweight a yardstick. The stick may break.
4. Remove the bag and weight. Rotate the yardstick so that it is on edge vertically.
5. Now hang the bag off the far end. The stick doesn't even bend.
6. And that's it.

What You Say

The subject of today's talk is *wait,* as in, "Wait your turn." "Any day now; I'm waiting." "Have you been waiting long?"

In the book of Psalms the words *wait* and *waiting* are used more than 15 times. David surely wants us to remember to wait on God, doesn't he? Here's one of those verses—"Wait on the LORD, and keep his way." That is Psalm 37:34. Waiting is a good thing. While we're waiting we are keeping God's ways, learning more of his will for us, and drawing closer to him. We're not just sitting there being bored.

The kind of wait we're talking about is spelled w-a-i-t. This day and age I'm not sure we're as good about waiting as they were back in David's day. We're bop-bopping here and zig-zagging there. We may think of that wait as being spelled w-e-i-g-h-t, like a weight hanging on a string . . . or this bag hanging off of this yardstick. *(Show both.)* In the bag I have a Bible, because the Bible is where it tells us to wait. What I'll do is tie the bag on the end of the yardstick. *(Hold stick flat horizontally.)* See how the stick bends way over from the weight? That's the way some people think waiting on God will do to us—weigh us down, slow us up, bend us over from the boredom.

But *(turn stick with edge vertically)* waiting on God never pulls us down. Check out the yardstick now. See, not a bend or a bow in it. That's because waiting on God doesn't slow us down. It builds us up, makes us stronger, and helps us accomplish more in this life. In short, when it comes to God—to wait is great.

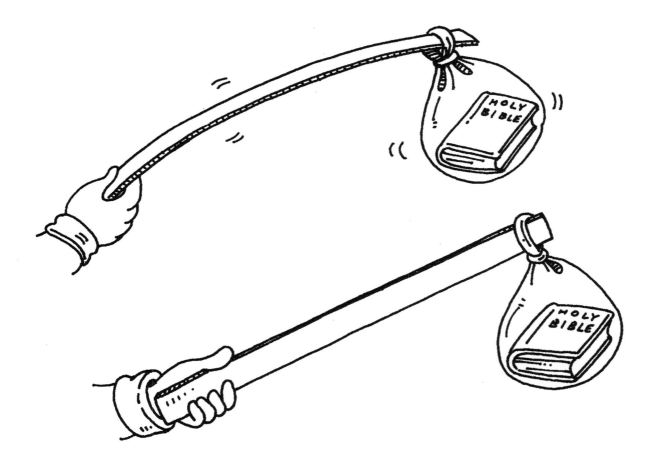

Blur and a Whir

Psalm 39:12a
Hear my prayer, LORD, listen to my cry for help.

What's Gonna Happen
You're going to make a humming cardboard spinner.

The How Behind the Wow
Energy from the winding string powers the spinner. Air moving through the holes creates the whirring noise.

What You Need
Piece of cardboard

Pencil

Nail (medium size)

String

Duct tape

CD

Scissors

Coffee-stirrer straw

Hot glue gun and sticks or white school glue

Markers (optional)

What You Do
1. Try to use a thin, strong cardboard. Set the CD or similar circle on the cardboard and trace a circle. Cut out the circle.
2. Near the center of the circle, mark two dots with the pencil ¼" to ⅜" apart. Punch through these marks with the nail. Use the nail to enlarge these holes enough for a coffee-stirrer straw to fit through.
3. Cut two small sections off of the straw. Each section should be approximately half an inch long. Push the straws through the holes. Hot glue them in place.
4. Cut a length of string that is five feet long. (I use a cotton string that is slightly thicker than kite string.) Thread the string through the straws and tie the string into a loop.
5. Wrap a small piece of duct tape around the knot. Also, wrap a two-inch piece of duct tape around the opposite end of the string from the knot. These wrapped duct tape strips will become handles.
6. Use the single hole punch to punch six holes around the perimeter of the cardboard circle.
7. Operate the spinner by holding the duct tape pieces in each hand. Begin twirling the spinner in a loop out in front of you. This will wind the string up. After a bit, stop the twirling. As the circle begins unwinding, pull outward on the handles. This accelerates the spinning. When the spinning speeds up, allow your hands to move inward. Then as the spinning slows, pull outward again. This will speed the circle up in the opposite direction. The spinning circle will make a whirring noise. The markers are for decorative purposes, if you choose.

What You Say

David used all of his senses when he experienced God. Our five senses are hearing, taste, smell, touch, and sight. We read verses like Psalm 34:8, "Taste and see that the LORD is good." And we have today's verse, Psalm 39:12, which says, "Hear my prayer, LORD, listen to my cry for help."

Hearing is such an important sense. Just imagine if I were saying Psalm 23 right now, but no sound was coming out. *(Mouth—but do not say aloud—"The Lord is my shepherd, I lack nothing. He makes me lie down in green pastures.")* See, it's not the same when we can't hear. Just one more thing to be thankful for every day.

So in honor of the word *hear* and the 45 plus times it appears in the book of Psalms, I've got a little hearing thing today. Here it is. *(Show spinner.)* I'm going to hold it by these little handles I've made, and I'm going to wind it up a bit. Here we go. Not much sound yet, is there? It'll come. What I do is pull on the strings, then let the spinner have slack. When it is about spun down, I pull once more, then let it have slack again. Pull and slack; pull and slack. Let's pick up speed . . . and faster. Ah, there we are. How about that?

You know what that *whirr* sounds like to me? It sounds like the word *wow!* Hear it? *Wow! Wow!* That's what people are going to say about you and your walk with the Lord.

I think I could keep doing this all day, whirring one way, then the other. But I suppose all good hearing things have to end. I'll let it ease down and stop. But, hey, be glad your hearing isn't going to stop. Nor will God's. When David said, "Hear my prayer, LORD," that could be our prayer also. Our hearing may come and go, but God's hearing is always totally perfect. And he hears our every prayer. So be thankful for your hearing and especially for God's hearing. Anybody want to try this *wow* thing?

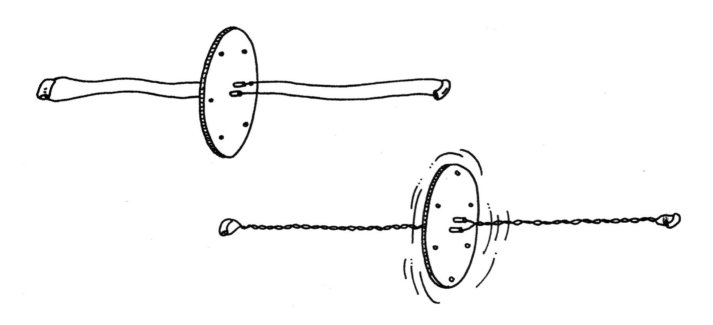

The Domino Effect

Psalm 40:8a
I desire to do your will, my God; your law is within my heart.

What's Gonna Happen
You're going to slide (or not) some dominoes down a tilted metal pan.

The How Behind the Wow
Friction is a force that opposes motion. Friction is created by bumps on adjacent surfaces, causing the surfaces to drag against each other. The more bumps there are, the greater the friction.

What You Need
Metal baking pan

Sandpaper (medium to large grain)

Scissors

Tape

6 dominoes

What You Do
1. Turn the pan upside down. You'll be working on the bottom.
2. Cover half of the pan (widthwise) with sandpaper. Use the scissors to cut the sandpaper to size. Tape the sandpaper in place.
3. Put three dominoes on the sandpaper and three on the metal. All six dominoes should be lined up along one of the edges of the pan.
4. Slowly lift up the edge of the pan. Soon, some of the dominoes will begin to slide across the pan. Keep lifting until all the dominoes have slid. The hypothesis here is that all of the "metal" dominoes will be gone before the "sandpaper" dominoes slide.

What You Say

The subject today is inspiration. When people inspire us, it makes us want to be good and do good. In the Bible, one of my main sources of inspiration is David. There were times he stumbled and times he bumbled. But there were so many times he was right on track and was humbled. We can read about his heart in the book of Psalms. Take Psalm 40:8, for instance. He says, "I desire to do your will, my God; your law is within my heart." Doing God's will was at the very top of David's to-do list. Hopefully, it is at the top of ours also.

Speaking of doing God's will, let's take a look at this domino pan. You'll notice there is sandpaper on one side, while it's slick on the other. What we're going to do is place these six dominoes along this edge close to me—three on the sandpaper, three on the metal. I'm going to pick up this side and let the dominoes slide down toward you. Which dominoes do you think will slide first? *(Encourage answers.)* Good answers.

(As you prepare to lift the pan . . .) The dominoes represent God's will for us. The surfaces? Well, they represent people. Some people welcome God's will in their lives; others resist like crazy. Why would they do that? Who knows? Maybe they think they know more than God. Anyhow, if the dominoes slide down easily, that's a good thing. Let's find out.

(Tilt pan. As dominoes begin to slide . . .) And those are the kind of people we want to be—embracing and chasing God's will. Let's not be like these *(point to the dominoes that are still on)* who are resisting with all their might, 'cause that's just not right.

Deep Calls to Deep

Psalm 42:7a
Deep calls to deep in the roar of your waterfalls.

What's Gonna Happen
You're going to make a simple, but effective, underwater viewer.

The How Behind the Wow
Your tin can viewer will enable you to push through a layer of soap suds, allowing you to see the bottom of a small tub of water. The cans are important. The big deal, though, is clear plastic wrap that's underwater.

What You Need
2 tin cans, same size
Book
Liquid dish soap
Clear plastic wrap
Water
Poster board
Scissors

Plastic tub (shoe box size)
Rubber band
Spoon
Duct tape
Can opener
Marker
Metal objects (coins, silverware, nails, paper clips, screws, etc.)

What You Do
1. Remove labels from the cans and use the can opener to cut both ends off the cans.
2. Duct tape the cans together, end to end.
3. Tear off a piece of clear plastic wrap. Place the wrap across one end of your "can tube." Use the rubber band to hold the wrap in place. Gently stretch the plastic wrap tight. Tear or cut off excess.
4. Place the metal objects into the tub. The book is to be placed in front of the tub so the objects can't be seen from the side.
5. On the poster, use the marker to list the objects. While a volunteer later does the sea hunt, you'll hold the poster up for your audience.
6. Run warm water into the plastic tub. As the tub is filling, squirt about ¼ cup of liquid dish soap into the water. Stir with the spoon as the tub is filling. You want the tub to be at least half full of water. There should be two inches of suds on top of the water. It's okay to have more. If you don't have enough suds, add more soap and stir.
7. Push the tin can viewer (wrap end down) through the soap suds into the water. You will need to slosh the viewer sideways to let the water push the soap off of the clear wrap. As you look down through the open end, you now have a window

through the soap suds. By moving the viewer around, you should easily be able to see the kinds and number of objects on the bottom of the tub.

8. You will need to freshen up the soap suds for your presentation.

What You Say

There's an interesting verse in one of the psalms. It's found in Psalm 42:7 and it says, "Deep calls to deep in the roar of your waterfalls." Hmm, wonder what that phrase—deep calls to deep—means? Any ideas? *(Accept all answers.)* Maybe it means that the deep things of God call out to the deepest part of our soul. See? Deep calls to deep.

Thing is, there are many distractions between us and God. I'll show you what I mean. Let's say this plastic tub of water represents God. Here in my hand I have a penny and nickel. *(Show these.)* Watch, I'll drop them into the water. Now they are at the bottom with some other things that I already put there. All those things at the bottom of the tub represent the deep things of God—the important things like his ideas and thoughts, his ways and will. You and I really want to connect with God on that level.

There's a problem, however. We can't see those deep things because of the distractions. The book in the front keeps us from looking in the side and the soap suds keep us from seeing straight down. What we need is some help. Kids, the help we need is in the form of a sharper focus. And that's what this tin can viewer does. *(Show viewer.)* It helps us look down through the soap—the distractions—and see things down deep. Would one of you like to try this?

Okay, here's what you do. Push the end with plastic wrap down through the soap and look through the open end. You may have to slosh the tube back and forth a bit to get soap suds off of the wrap. That's okay. Once you do that, though, you have it made. Just slowly move around and tell us what you see. I have a list of the objects for everyone to see. That way they'll know what a great job you are doing.

(Hold up poster so others can follow along. You're now the cheerleader for your volunteer. When he has finished . . .) Great job! Way to go. You found three pennies, a fork, a nickel, and two nails. Did our underwater viewer help you focus? *(Allow answers.)* Yes, it did. And, everybody, that's the way focusing on God works. We learn things we would never otherwise even think about. Above all, God becomes our best friend. So let's keep our focus on God, as deep calls to deep.

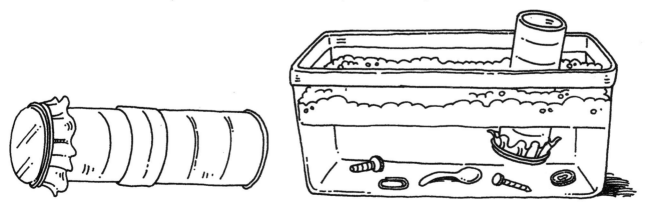

Disappearing Engineering

Psalm 44:8a
In God we make our boast all day long.

What's Gonna Happen
You're going to make some water disappear, then reappear.

The How Behind the Wow
In many diapers there is a grainy powder called sodium polyacrylate. This is a synthetic polymer which can absorb many times its weight in water. The powder is sprinkled into the cotton rectangle at the bottom of diapers. As the powder absorbs, um, liquid, the powder turns into a gel.

What You Need
Spoon

Clear plastic glass

4 Styrofoam® cups (small)

Permanent marker

Scissors

Plate

2 Luvs® Ultra Leakguards or other good diapers (The small print on the package should say something like, "If you notice gel-like material on your baby's skin, don't be alarmed." Save unused diapers for the Diaper Diamonds demo if you haven't done it yet.)

What You Do
1. Set the plate out. Do step 3 over the plate.
2. With the marker, write "YOU" on the clear plastic glass. Write "JESUS" on one of the foam cups and write "GOD" on the other.
3. Lay the diaper on the plate. Use the scissors to cut out the rectangular center section of the diaper. Cut just a bit into the center itself.
4. As you are cutting, a grainy powder will begin falling out onto the plate. This is a good thing. When you are finished cutting, open the center section over the plate and gently rub out as much of the powder as you can. Toss away any little cotton fluffs.
5. In the cups:
   a. Fill the GOD cup about a fourth of the way with water.
   b. Fill the clear YOU glass a fourth of the way with water also.
   c. Put the powder from the diaper into the JESUS cup. Do not put water in the JESUS cup.
6. Pour the water from the YOU glass into the JESUS cup. Give the JESUS cup 30 seconds, then turn it upside down. No water comes out.
7. That pretty much ends the doing part of your practice. All the rest will be built into the flow of the talk. Discard gel in the trash, not the sink.

8. Prepare everything fresh for your talk, including new foam cups. All should be set up before you begin your talk.

9. Be sure to read over **What You Say** ahead of time.

What You Say

Do you know what the word *boast* means? *(Accept any answers.)* It means to brag. When we boast about ourselves, we are pumping ourselves up before other people. Psalm 44:8 has the answer to this. That verse says, "In God we make our boast all day long."

Above Psalm 44 it says that it was written by the sons of Korah. Well, Korah must have had some pretty smart boys, 'cause they got it right. If we're going to boast, let's not brag about ourselves, but about God.

And today we have an advantage they didn't have in the days when the book of Psalms was written. Since those days, Jesus has come into the world. We can brag to him and he will pass our boast on to God. How about that? The Bible says that Jesus is sitting at the right hand of God. Doesn't get much closer than that.

Here, I'll show you what I mean. See this clear glass? That represents you. And that water in the glass? That's your boast about God. Along with the YOU glass I have two foam cups. Look, one of them is labeled "Jesus" and the other is labeled "God."

I'll start by pouring the water from the YOU glass into the JESUS cup. *(Do this.)* That's us passing our boast about God on to Jesus. *(Give the powder a few seconds to absorb the water. While all is taking place, continue talking.)*

Now one thing we know is that Jesus and God are just like that. *(Hold two fingers together.)* During his time on earth, Jesus never did anything without checking with his Father first. Still today in Heaven, the love they have for each other is an amazing thing. Remember, Jesus is sitting at the right hand of God. So when Jesus gets your boast about God, he just says, "Sure, I'll be glad to pass it on." And with that he passes along your boast to God. *(Turn the JESUS cup upside down.)* What? Where did your boast go? *(Look around.)*

(Hold up the GOD cup.) Oh, wait. Here it is. He's already passed it along to God. *(Pour water from the GOD cup into the YOU glass.)* God says thank you so much for boasting about him. Anytime you want, you can boast about him again.

Soft Pop

Psalm 46:6a,10a

Nations are in uproar, kingdoms fall. . . . "Be still, and know that I am God."

What's Gonna Happen

You will pop two balloons—one with a loud pop, the other quietly.

The How Behind the Wow

Rubber is a natural polymer material made of long, thin molecules. When balloons are inflated, the molecules stretch away from each other. If a pencil is stuck in the side of the balloon, the balloon instantly pops. However, at either end of a balloon, the molecules are still overlapped atop each other. This is why the ends of balloons are darker in color. Sticking a pencil into the balloon near the knot does not result in a *pop*. Instead, air can be squeezed out quietly.

What You Need

12" balloons
Sharpened pencil
Permanent marker

What You Do

1. Inflate and tie off a balloon.
2. Pull the knot of the balloon upward. While stretching the knot of the balloon, stick the pencil into the darker-colored area near the knot. The balloon shouldn't pop. In fact, you will need to pull the pencil sideways in the hole you've created. This will stretch the opening and allow air to escape from the balloon.
3. This is pretty much it. Practice as you feel necessary.
4. For your presentation, inflate and tie off two balloons just before your talk. Use the marker to write on the balloons. On one balloon, write "UPROAR." On the other balloon, write "BE STILL."

What You Say

Hey, there. I've got two balloons today. *(Show balloons and pencil.)* You'd be amazed at the things that two balloons and a pencil can teach us about God. We're taking a look at Psalm 46. In verse six it says this, "Nations are in uproar, kingdoms fall." That's the way things were back in the day. And do you know what? They still are. Seems like there's always something going on somewhere in the world. That's why I have the word *uproar* written on this balloon. *(Show balloon.)*

If I were to stick this pencil into the UPROAR balloon, what do you think would happen? *(Allow answers.)* Okay, I think I'm with you. It would cause an uproar. Well, let's see if you're right. *(Pop the UPROAR balloon loudly.)* Hmm, I'd say that you were definitely correct.

Also in Psalm 46 is a different kind of verse. Psalm 46:10 says, "Be still, and know that I am God." Being still is the opposite of uproar. Which is why I have this other balloon. *(Show the BE STILL balloon.)* Being still before God is a good thing. When we're still and quiet we can have neat thoughts about God. He likes that and so do we.

This time with the pencil, I'm going to soft pop the balloon. Instead of an explosion there will just be a little *bump* as the pencil enters the balloon. After that I'll squeeze the air out of the balloon, like this. *(Soft pop the BE STILL balloon. When balloon is deflated, continue.)*

See what I mean? Uproar—*kapow!* Be still—*psssh.* So no matter what is going on around us in the world, let's find a place where we can be still and know that he is God.

Air Chair

Psalm 47:8

God reigns over the nations; God is seated on his holy throne.

What's Gonna Happen

You're going to turn a new trash bag into an air chair.

The How Behind the Wow

Air is matter. It has mass and definitely occupies space, as you will demonstrate. What some might classify as an empty trash bag turns out to not be empty at all. It's full of an invisible matter we know as air.

What You Need

2 new white trash bags
Marker
Duct tape

What You Do

1. Tear off three inches of the duct tape. Now tear it lengthwise into thirds. You will only need one of these strips for your air chair.
2. Place a strip of the duct tape on the edge of a table or somewhere handy.
3. Completely open the trash bag. Hold it out in front of you and spin around in a full 360° circle to fill the bag full of air.
4. Quickly close and twist the bag shut.
5. This next part is easy, but I've figured out 15 different ways to goof it up. You've now got about a half bag of air. You want to wrap the duct tape around the twisted part to keep the air in the bag. But you don't want to get the tape stuck someplace else on the bag, tear the bag, or let the air out. So:
   a. either have one of the kids do the taping while you hold the bag, or
   b. be sure you allow plenty of space for the duct tape.
6. Use the marker to write "AIR CHAIR" on the bag.
7. Now that you've practiced all of this, you'll start from scratch for your talk.
8. Be sure to have a piece of duct tape already torn off when you begin.

What You Say

It is hard for us to visualize God. We can't see him or touch him, but we know he's there. He's right here with us and at the same time he's sitting on his throne in Heaven. In a way, God reminds me of air. Air is all around us. We can't see it, but we certainly don't let that stop us from breathing air 24-7. You might say, "God and air are everywhere."

It's an awesome thing to picture God on his throne. In the book of Psalms the writers did this. Here's what Psalm 47:8 says, "God reigns over the nations; God is seated on his holy throne."

So with that picture in our minds—the picture of God seated on his holy throne—we're going to return to our idea of "God and air are everywhere." And what we're going to do is make an air chair! Here we go. First, I'll unfold this brand new trash bag. Totally empty, correct? Yes, it is. (Snap it out all the way open.) Now I'll spin myself around in a circle, holding the bag out in front of me. In the process I'll scoop a whole bunch of air into the bag. That's kinda fun. (Spin, then quickly twist bag closed.) Not empty anymore, is it? No way. It's got lots of air in it.

To keep that air in there, I'm going to use this little piece of duct tape around our twisted end. I'll tape it up tight. There, that's done. And finally, with this marker I'll write "AIR CHAIR" on the bag. Would anybody like to sit on our air chair? (Would they! Just watch.)

So remember, the point of our air chair is to remind us that God and air are everywhere. Wish I had just one more word that rhymes with air and everywhere. Hmm (snap fingers), I've got it—prayer. God and air are everywhere; he's as close as a prayer. That'll work.

Chair Spin Curve

Psalm 48:12-14a
Walk about Zion, go around her, count her towers
. . . that you may tell of them to the next generation.
For this God is our God for ever and ever.

What's Gonna Happen
You will spin a volunteer in a spinning chair. The volunteer will accelerate during the spin.

The How Behind the Wow
Radial acceleration occurs when objects move in a circle. The acceleration is toward the center of the circle. The tighter everything is toward the center, the faster the acceleration. So when your volunteer pulls the soup cans toward himself, he will go faster, just like ice skaters do when ending a routine.

What You Need
Spinning chair, such as an office-type chair, especially one that has a back
2 soup cans
Duct tape

What You Do
1. Make an impromptu seat belt out of two strips of duct tape. One strip is a yard long. Lay this on a table, sticky side up. On top of this, place a 24" strip of duct tape facing downward. Leave six inches of the first strip exposed at each end. These ends will stick to the back of the chair after the duct tape is placed around the volunteer.
2. Have a volunteer sit in the chair. Put the seat belt on snugly. Gotta have safety.
3. Have the volunteer hold a soup can in each hand. The volunteer should have his hands extended out sideways. This is the way the volunteer begins as you give the chair a firm but gentle spin. Part way through the spin you say, "Now." At this command the volunteer quickly pulls the soup cans in toward his chest. The chair will noticeably accelerate. You will see it; the volunteer will feel it. In your talk you'll explain step 3 before actually doing it.
4. I usually give two spins, the second to unwind the first.
5. If you have them available, small dumbbells (three or five pound sets) work better than soup cans.

What You Say

Sometimes you read the word *Zion* in the Bible. When the Bible talks about Zion, it's often talking about the city of Jerusalem. For more than 3,000 years, Jerusalem has been a city of major importance to the Jewish people. Zion is mentioned more than 35 times in the book of Psalms. That includes today's verses. They are Psalm 48:12-14 and they go like this, "Walk about Zion, go around her, count her towers . . . that you may tell of them to the next generation. For this God is our God for ever and ever."

"Going around Zion" is our theme today. The writer of Psalm 48 said to walk around Zion. I thought we might go a tad faster. For that reason I brought this spinning chair. Would someone—someone who doesn't get dizzy—like to be our volunteer to take a spin around Zion? *(Don't think you'll have any trouble finding customers.)* Excellent. Have a seat and we'll put this seat belt *(show duct tape)* around you. We believe in safety.

Now before I give you a spin, I want you to hold these soup cans straight out to your side. After I spin you, I'll say, "Now." When I do, quickly pull those cans in to your chest. That's going to speed up your tour of Zion. Got it? Good. Okay, hold those cans out to the side and here we go. *(Give the chair a spin.)* And, now! Whoa, did everybody see that acceleration? That was one quick tour around the walls of Zion. *(Stop the chair.)* Okay, one spin back the other way to unwind and we'll be good. Cans out and here we go.

(When done . . .) And so like the verse said, we've walked about Zion. Maybe we even got a speeding ticket. But here's the most important part. As verse 13 says, we will tell of what we've seen to the next generation. Why? The answer to that is in verse 14, "For this God is our God for ever and ever." Kids, we can know a million things in this life and none of them will be more important than knowing that truth. "This God is our God for ever and ever." Kind of makes you want to say, "Amen," doesn't it?

STICKY SIDE DOWN

STICKY SIDE UP

DUCT TAPE "SEAT BELT"

Time to Wash Up

Psalm 51:7b
Wash me, and I will be whiter than snow.

What's Gonna Happen
You're going to put some iodine on a white paper towel. Then you'll dip the towel into a glass of water. Like that, no stain will remain.

The How Behind the Wow
You will dip the iodine towel into a solution of OxiClean and warm water. The oxygen in the OxiClean reacts with the iodine stain, causing the stain to totally disappear. The towel will be as white as before.

What You Need
Clear glass
Water
Iodine
Thermos

OxiClean® Versatile Stain Remover Powder
White paper towels
Teaspoon

What You Do
1. Fill the glass half full of warm–hot water.
2. Stir in a large teaspoon of OxiClean.
3. Put several drops of iodine in the center of the white paper towel.
4. Loosely fold the paper towel. Hold the paper towel so that the iodine spots are at the bottom of the towel.
5. Dip the iodine spots into the glass of OxiClean and water solution. Within moments you will see bubbles as the oxygen reacts with the iodine. Shortly, you will be able to remove the paper towel. Squeeze it a bit to remove excess water, then unfold the towel to show its totally white appearance.
6. I'd plan on starting from scratch with your talk—pouring warm water from the thermos, etc. However, if time is of the essence, this demo will still work with water that has been sitting out. That way, you could already have the OxiClean mixed and ready to go.

What You Say

It's pretty interesting what you run across in the Bible from time to time. Actually, the Bible is interesting all the time. It's just that sometimes you see things that make you go, "Whoa." Well, we've got one of those "whoa" things today.

Psalm 51:7 says, "Wash me, and I will be whiter than snow." That's pretty straight up. Nothing "whoa" there, except for the comparison to snow. You see, Bible lands were mostly desert areas or close to it. You just don't hook up deserts and snow. I mean, can you imagine a guy staggering in off of the desert and saying, "I was doing okay out there on those burning sands until that snowstorm blew in"? I don't think so.

Obviously, however, they knew about snow. So when David had an oops in his life and wanted to be forgiven by God, he thought of the whitest thing he knew about—snow. "Wash me, and I will be whiter than snow." The idea is, "Lord, please forgive my sin as only you can do. Then I will be truly clean again, as clean as snow on the mountains."

To me, this brings to mind this paper towel. I imagine you were thinking of a paper towel also. The paper towel represents us. On this paper towel I'll put a few drops of iodine. *(Do this.)* That represents our sins, our oops, just like David's. That iodine leaves a stain, doesn't it? I'm thinking that's what sin must do in our souls. And we don't want that. God surely doesn't want it. So, what do we do? Well, we ask him to forgive us and cleanse us. That's what we do. *(Show water and OxiClean solution.)* That's what David did, back in the day.

Let's find out if it works. *(Gather up paper towel with stains at the bottom of the gather; dip into the solution.)* I'll just dip the paper towel a time or two, maybe swirl it around a little. And look! *(Take out paper towel, unfold, and display.)* The stains are all gone. The paper towel looks brand new.

And kids, it's the same way with God. When we go to him and ask, "Wash me, and I will be whiter than snow," he does just that. God is amazing.

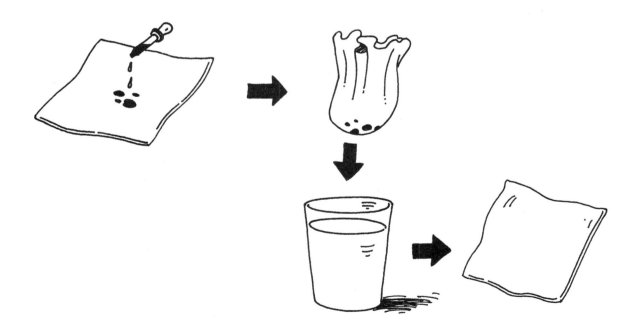

The Circle Won't Be Broken

Psalm 51:10a
Create in me a pure heart, O God.

What's Gonna Happen
You will make two foam board-flying rings, intentionally mess one up, then fly both of them.

The How Behind the Wow
Flying discs and rings get their stability from their rotation. Spinning is a neat thing. It creates rotational inertia. Thus, the spinning object stays in the same plane (orientation) as it flies.

What You Need
Foam board (stationery section at Walmart)
Markers
X-ACTO® knife #1
2 round objects with different diameters (mixing bowls, butter tubs, etc.)

What You Do
1. Place the foam board on a table or counter. You will make two identical flying rings from this board. The rings will be hollow on the inside.
2. Find two bowls or containers that are different sizes. Place the larger one (maybe a mixing bowl) on the foam board and trace around it.
3. Center the smaller container (butter tub, possibly) inside the first circle. There should be about a two-inch gap between the two circles. That will be the thickness of your flying ring. Trace around the smaller container. Remember to trace for two rings.
4. A #1 X-ACTO knife is perfect for cutting foam board. It's just sharp as all get-out; definitely not a tool or job for children.
5. Cut around both lines on each ring, giving two hollow rings.
6. Keep one of the rings as is. You can even color it up.
7. Use the X-ACTO knife to cut zigs, zags, and notches into the other ring. It will be recognizable as a ring, but that's about all.
8. Try gently throwing each ring indoors. There will be a difference in flight between the two. The larger your area, the more dramatic that difference will be. Okay, you're good to throw—uh, go. If you decide to sail the rings across the church, try not to conk anyone in the congregation.

What You Say

One thing about David, when he made mistakes in his life he would ask God to forgive him. Finally, he'd say things like Psalm 51:10, "Create in me a pure heart, O God."

A pure heart is a good thing for all of us to have. It reminds me of this homemade flying ring. *(Show the good ring.)* What do you think? I'm kind of proud of it 'cause I made it myself. And it actually works. That's the best thing of all. It's for indoors, so I'll throw it gently to one of you and you *gently* throw it back, okay? *(Couple of tosses.)*

Usually we don't think of hearts as being round like this. But let's just suppose this represents us with a clean heart. This flying ring is supposed to glide across the room and it does. As Christians we are supposed to be like Christ. He loves it when our hearts are pure.

But if folks aren't careful, their hearts may lose a bit of the desire to be like Jesus. Then it may not be too long *(pull out second ring)* before they become like this ring. *(Hold the two rings up for comparison.)* You can see what it's supposed to be, but it sure doesn't look like the good one, does it? Wonder if it will even fly. One way to find out. *(Toss second ring.)* Hmm, not so much. It kinda does and kinda doesn't.

And that is the story of the two rings. One looks like it's supposed to and does what it was meant for. The other—nope. The good news is, if you and I ever think we're slipping even a tiny notch away from God, we can pray that prayer of David's— "Create in me a clean heart, O God." And do you know what God will do? *(Allow answers.)* Exactly. *(Toss good ring.)* He'll create a clean heart within us.

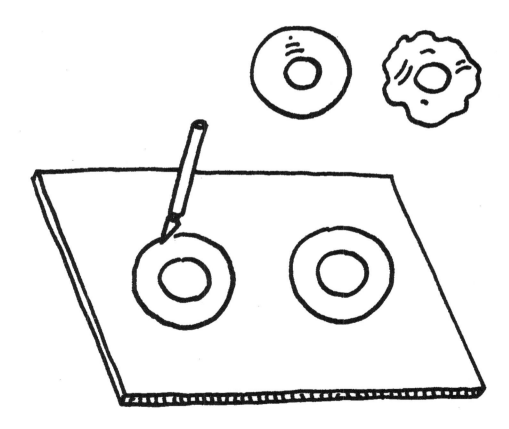

Shelter in the Storm

Psalm 55:8
I would hurry to my place of shelter, far from the tempest and storm.

What's Gonna Happen
You're going to make a tornado in a bottle.

The How Behind the Wow
When you spin the two bottles of water, you will create a vortex. A *vortex* is a spinning flow of fluids (liquids or gases). The pressure is less in the center of the vortex, just as it is in a tornado.

What You Need
2 clear 2-liter bottles
Blue food coloring
White school glue
Weight (book, etc.)

Water
Scissors
Electrical tape
Flat washer (1" outside diameter; ¼" or ½" inside diameter)

What You Do
1. Use the scissors to cut through the labels on the two-liter bottles. While holding the glue areas of the labels under running hot water, pull the labels off of the bottles.
2. Put some glue around the mouth of one bottle. Set the flat washer on the glue. Place a weight on the washer.
3. Put seven drops of blue food coloring in the second bottle. Fill this second bottle three-fourths full of water. Put some glue around the top of this bottle.
4. Turn the first bottle upside down and set the washer onto the glue of bottle two. If possible, place a weight on top to help things stick.
5. When dry, the two bottles will be somewhat stuck to the washer. To secure this junction, wrap electrical tape around the tops of the bottles and the washer. This is a shaky connection, to say the least.
6. To make this work, it's important to get the next two steps right.
7. Place your left hand beneath the bottom bottle. Wrap your right hand around the junction between the bottles. **Be sure your thumb is facing downward.**
8. Turn everything over. Now your left hand is at the top and your right hand is facing so that the thumb is up. While holding tightly with both hands, give the two bottles a couple of hard spins. This will start the tornado going.
9. I wouldn't let kids do this demo. Invariably, they'll break the connection at the washer and you may have blue water going everywhere!

What You Say

Let's talk about storms today, okay? Storms and shelter. Can anybody think of a kind of storm? *(You'll get 'em all most likely—thunderstorms, hurricanes, rainstorms, tornadoes, and more.)* Wow, you all did really well. You know your storms.

People knew about storms in Bible days too. Listen to what David says in Psalm 55:8, "I would hurry to my place of shelter, far from the tempest and storm." You see, storms can be of all kinds. They can be weather storms like we just named. Or they can be storms between people, between nations, even storms just within ourselves. David, though, had found the answer. God was David's place of shelter far away from any storms.

So here we are today, needing a shelter in the storm too. And do you know what? The same shelter that David found is still available. God is still there for us. Or maybe I should say, still here for us. Isn't that a great feeling? The same God that David called on for help and comfort is here for us as well.

With that in mind, I thought I'd show you a storm today. It's my "tornado in a bottle." *(Show tornado bottles.)* I'm thinking these bottles are the very best place for a tornado. Here's what a tornado looks like. *(Spin one up.)* See what I mean? There's our tornado. It would be nice if all the storms stayed in a bottle. Sometimes, however, storms get out of the bottle. That's when we need a place of shelter.

And that brings us back to the point of today's verse. If you ever need a friend—a forever friend—run to the arms of Jesus. He will always be your shelter in the storm.

Hey, wanna see one more tornado? Okay, here we go.

Note: If you want something more permanent, do an Internet search for "tornado tube" and you will find many sites that sell inexpensive connectors. One site is www.stevespanglerscience.com. The price in 2011 is $2.50. (Standard Publishing does not necessarily endorse the contents of web sites mentioned here.)

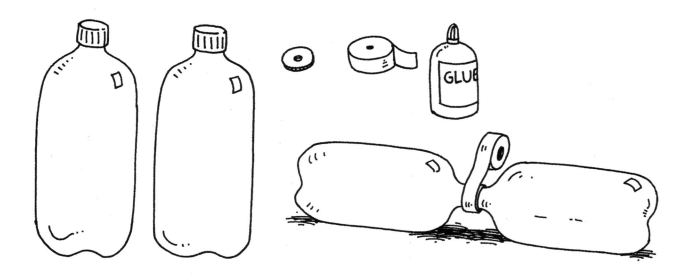

Trust Is a Must

Psalm 56:3, 4a

When I am afraid, I put my trust in you. In God, whose word I praise—in God I trust and am not afraid.

What's Gonna Happen

You're going to snatch the props from beneath a stack of coins. Instead of scattering, they'll fall into a glass.

The How Behind the Wow

Matter has mass. This mass gives objects inertia. *Inertia* is a Greek word that means "lazy." It could also mean keep on keeping on. If an object is sitting still, because of its inertia, it basically wants to keep on staying still. If it is moving, it wants to keep on moving. The coins, being still, want to remain still. So when the bottom is removed, they fall straight down.

What You Need

Drinking glass (not plastic)
Ruler
Pennies and nickels

Scissors
3 x 6 rectangle cut from a cereal box
Quarter

What You Do

1. Using the scissors, cut out the front of the cereal box. Use the ruler to measure a 3 x 6 inch rectangle on this cardboard. Cut the rectangle out with the scissors.
2. Lay the cardboard rectangle on top of the glass. Instead of being centered, more of the long part should extend toward you.
3. Stack 10 coins on the card. These should be stacked above the center of the glass.
4. Hold onto the glass with one hand. With your other hand, grab the portion of the card sticking out your way. Snatch the card from beneath the coins. As they say at Silver Dollar City in Branson, Missouri, "This ain't no time for lollygagging, boys." Pour on the speed. All of the coins will fall into the glass.
5. Practice a few more times, increasing the number of coins, either on the same stack or by making new stacks.
6. Take all things for your talk. Don't forget the quarter.

What You Say

Have you ever read our money? Really. You can read money. It has words all over it. *(Hold up a quarter.)* Take this quarter, for example. The tails side is full of words. On the other hand, the heads side has just five words. All five words are very important. At the top it says, "Liberty." Then down toward the bottom, "In God we trust." We hope everybody who reads those words believes in liberty and really does trust in God, don't we?

Listen to these words about trusting God. They come from Psalm 56:3, 4, "When I am afraid, I put my trust in you. In God, whose word I praise—in God I trust and am not afraid." Aren't those great words? They may be the very words that inspired the words on our money. Trusting in God is a good thing 'cause if anything ever goes wrong, he's there for us.

I'll show you what I mean. Here's a glass. That glass will stand for God. Next, we have a card. That would be a little landscape that represents things we put our trust in besides God. On top of the card I'll stack some coins. Remember, each coin says, "In God we trust." Those coins are like us, trusting in God. Now as long as everything is cool, those coins are standing steady, just like us. But what if something comes along to upend us? Well, we'll show you. Keep your eyes on the coins. *(Snatch card.)* How about that? Even when the props were snatched from under us, we fell into the arms of God. Because we trusted him.

Let's do it one more time, shall we, with even more trust. *(Stack a bunch of coins and wow the crowd.)* So you see, there's no such thing as trusting too much. In fact, we could say, "Everything is good, just relax. Because God has got your back."

Leaning on Jesus

Psalm 62:3
How long will you assault me? Would all of you throw me down—this leaning wall, this tottering fence?

What's Gonna Happen
You will lean a soda pop can on its bottom edge, so that it stands at a tilt.

The How Behind the Wow
This demo is about the center of gravity and two balance points. Too much water in the pop can and the can tilts over. Too little water, or no water, and the can also falls over. But a half cup of water proves to be just the right amount. The center of gravity is above the bottom rims of the pop can, thus the can balances as it leans. Another factor which helps this demo work is that there are two contact points at the bottom of the can. The can balances when both of these are touching the table.

What You Need
Empty soda pop can
Water
Measuring cup

What You Do
1. Measure between ⅓ and ½ cup of water in the measuring cup.
2. Pour the water into the empty pop can.
3. Gently lean the can over sideways till it is resting on both contact points. Gradually release the can, testing to see if it will remain balanced. All should be good.
4. For your talk, leave the water in the pop can.

What You Say

(Begin with the can sitting in plain view on a table. The half cup of water should already be in the pop can.) Today we have a verse with two question marks in it. The verse is Psalm 62:3. It goes like this, "How long will you assault me? Would all of you throw me down—this leaning wall, this tottering fence?"

David is asking everybody, "What's up, y'all? How come you're looking at me like that? What do you think I am—a leaning, old wall? You'd better check your own self. I'm good to go."

And kids, David was good to go. In verse one of Psalm 62 he had already stated, "My soul finds rest in God alone." Then in verse two David had added, "He alone is my rock and my salvation." That's where we catch up with David in verse three, telling the world that he and God are tight. He says, "I'm not a leaning wall about to fall down and go boom. God is my strength; that's what counts."

To honor David's commitment to God, I have a soda can. Soda cans have a nice round base. They are made to stand straight up. But, you know what? If we tilt the can a little at a time *(do this),* before you know it we can let the can go. Look, it leans there by itself.

So my friends, the next time you happen to see a soda can standing just so, not falling over or standing back up, remember what David knew. God is the source of our rest and strength. We're not leaning walls or tottering fences. We are children of the King. That is a fact we can always stand strong upon.

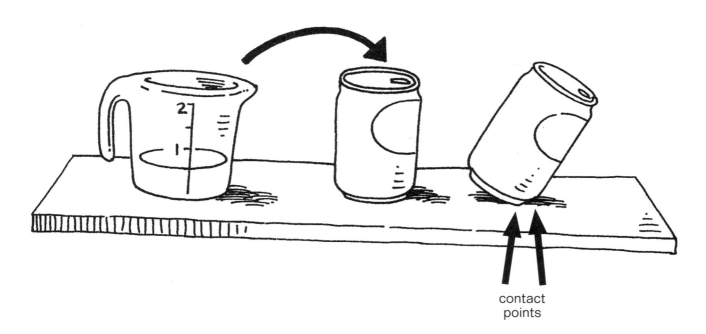

contact
points

Park Your Marker

Psalm 62:7
My salvation and my honor depend on God.

What's Gonna Happen
You will make the neatest little teeter-totter.

The How Behind the Wow
The way this will work is this: You'll have equal amounts of water in two cups. These will balance on a paint-stirring stick. When you push down with a marker on the water (only) in one of the cups, the teeter-totter will tip downward in that direction. The concept is that no two pieces of matter can occupy the same place at the same time. Therefore, the marker pushes aside some of the water. The marker becomes part of the weight on that side of the teeter-totter. Consequently, that end of the teeter-totter goes downward.

What You Need
2 clear plastic glasses

Pencil with hexagonal sides

Marker

Water

Paint-stirring stick

What You Do
1. Fill each glass two-thirds full of water.
2. Place the pencil on a table.
3. Center the paint-stirring stick across the pencil. Place a glass of water on either end of the stick. Try to get these to balance so that the stick is not touching the table. This is next to impossible, but it doesn't matter. The stick doesn't have to be off the table on both ends. You only want the stick to be as close as possible to balancing. *(In a pinch, a flat ruler will work in place of the paint-stirring stick, but the stick is still the best.)*
4. One glass will rest on the table; the other will be upraised. Lower the blunt end of the marker into the water of the upraised glass. *(Don't push the marker all the way down against the bottom of the glass.)* When the marker goes deep enough into the water, this higher glass will begin to tip downward. Take the marker out. If you're *very* close to being balanced, this end will stay down. That way you will then be able to push down on the other end next. That's the hope and the plan—to be able to alternate pushing down on either glass of water.
5. Have everything set up as precisely as possible for your talk.

What You Say

One of my favorite verses in the book of Psalms is 62:7. That verse says, "My salvation and my honor depend on God." The verse reminds me that our walk with God has two parts—the beginning and the journey. Our salvation is the beginning, that time when we ask Jesus into our heart. Then the journey is our honor—how we live our lives. Listen to Psalm 62:7 again: "My salvation and my honor depend on God."

Do you get it? Both parts of our walk with Christ—the beginning and the journey—depend on God. He is the one who is there for us—encouraging us, comforting us, guiding us. Our salvation and our honor really do depend on him.

Brings to mind this stick I have balanced with a glass of water on each end. Here's a question for you. You'll notice one side is touching the table; the other side is barely in the air. I have a marker here. If I put the marker into the upraised glass, just pushing against the water and not the bottom of the glass, what will happen? Will the glass stay put or will it go down? *(Accept all answers.)* Hmm, all good answers. Let's find out, shall we?

(Put in the marker till the glass responds.) How about that! The glass went down and it stayed down. Let's try the marker on the other side. *(Do this.)* And look. Now the other side goes down. Both sides depend on the marker, don't they?

And that is the way I see Psalm 62:7. Both parts of our walk with God depend on him. Our salvation depends on God *(push one side down)*, and our honor depends on God *(push other side down)*. And when we have them both, we are surely living a balanced life.

But First, the Thirst

Psalm 63:1a
You, God, are my God, earnestly I seek you; I thirst for you.

What's Gonna Happen
You're going to challenge a volunteer to eat six crackers in one minute. Not going to happen.

The How Behind the Wow
The crackers absorb the saliva in the mouth. The dryness makes it virtually impossible for anyone (adults or children) to eat the six crackers in one minute. Check it out.

What You Need
Saltine crackers, not saltless   Plate
Stopwatch, watch, or clock   Glasses of water

What You Do
1. Try the six-crackers-in-one-minute challenge yourself, just to see how close you get.
2. As you begin your talk, set six crackers on the plate and set out a glass of water. Don't want anyone to choke.

Be sure to have a glass of water for your volunteer.

What You Say

Sometimes the Bible uses the most amazing words about our search for God. It will say things like, "I cry out to God most high" (Psalm 57:2). Isn't that a great picture? To "cry out" for God? That's when we know that we really want to find God. Other times the Bible talks about us hungering for God. Hungering for God is searching deep to meet him.

And then we have today's verse from Psalm 63:1, "You, God, are my God, earnestly I seek you; I thirst for you." Cry out, hunger, thirst—all words that talk about us really wanting to connect with God. Thirst is a powerful feeling. We've all been thirsty before. Sometimes we get really thirsty. That's when nothing is better than a cold drink of water. David is saying that exact thing: that sometimes he just really thirsted for God.

So today in honor of thirst, I have a challenge for someone. You'll notice on this plate that I have six crackers. I'm going to let you take one cracker at a time and eat it as fast as you can. Then take another, and another. Your goal is to eat all six of the crackers in one minute. Anybody want to take the cracker-eating challenge? *(Choose a volunteer.)*

Okay, here we go. Take your first cracker. I'll start the timer when you start eating. Oh, and here is a glass of water just in case. We don't want you to start choking. *(Begin timing. When the minute is up . . .)* Hey, not too bad. You ate ____ crackers. That was good. You see, the reason it's so hard to eat all six is that the crackers absorb the saliva in our mouth. The drier our mouth becomes, the harder it is to swallow the crackers. All we do is just chew and chew as the time passes. Even grown-ups can't eat six crackers in one minute. Try it on your parents sometime.

And if you do try this on someone, remember the point. As we eat those crackers our mouth gets drier and drier. And so, we get thirstier and thirstier. We really want water. *(Hold up glass.)* David says that's the way we should want God. With that, I'll hand another glass of water to our great volunteer.

Spring into Missions

Psalm 67:1, 2
May God be gracious to us and bless us and make his face shine on us—so that your ways may be known on earth, your salvation among all nations.

What's Gonna Happen
You're going to launch a notebook spring across the room.

The How Behind the Wow
There are a couple of things going on here: (1) Once compressed, springs have the property of being able to return to their original position. This is known as elasticity. (2) Work is done on the spring to compress it. This gives the spring potential energy. Releasing the spring gets the work back out in the form of kinetic energy.

What You Need
Inexpensive notebook
Dowel rod (either ¼" or ⁵⁄₁₆" diameter; standard 36" length)
Wire snips

What You Do
1. The first thing you need to do is remove all of the notebook paper from the spring. You also want to remove the two covers. Take it easy when doing this, so you don't overstretch the spring. Use the wire snips to cut off the hooks from both ends of the spring.
2. Hold the dowel rod in your left hand. Have your hand at about the middle of the stick. Hold the dowel so that your left thumbnail is pushing straight down toward the stick. This thumbnail will be the stop and launching pad for the spring.
3. Slide the spring onto the dowel until it meets your left thumb. Compress the spring against the left thumb, then release your right hand. The coiled spring should launch off of the dowel rod. I say *should* because it's not automatic. If it doesn't launch, try:
   a. launching again, being sure to keep your left thumb vertically compressed against the dowel rod, or
   b. stretching the spring out beforehand. This creates a greater difference between the resting position and the compressed position of the spring. This will help.

What You Say

I found an interesting verse in the book of Psalms. Two verses, actually. The first verse starts a thought, then the second verse finishes it. The verses are Psalm 67:1, 2 and they go like this, "May God be gracious to us and bless us and make his face shine on us—so that your ways may be known on earth, your salvation among all nations."

Did you catch the two verses? The first verse says, "May God be gracious to us and bless us." Everybody wants God's blessings. People pray for that all the time. Ah, but then the second verse tells us the point of his blessings. And it turns out it's not about us. The second verse says, "That your ways may be known on earth, your salvation among all nations." You see? The point of the blessings is not just for us to be happier or healthier or richer. No, the point of the blessings is that God's name and ways may be spread around the world.

So with that in mind, I think we should all spring into missions. *Missions* is a word that means spreading the gospel, both near and far. To show you how that looks, I have a wooden stick. It's called a dowel rod. And I have a notebook spring, without the notebook, of course. I'll first stretch the spring out a bit. Now I'll slide it down the dowel rod, pray for God's blessings, then "spring" into missions. *(Launch the spring away from kids—hopefully, long distance. Pick up spring, restretch, and reload.)*

So remember, it's great to pray for God's blessings. Let's just keep in mind that he wants to bless us so that we can spread the word about his goodness. The more we spread the word, the more he will bless us. And the more he blesses us, the more we spread the word. It's a never-ending circle of springing *(launch the spring again)* into missions.

Diaper Diamonds

Psalm 68:14

When the Almighty scattered the kings in the land, it was like snow fallen on Mount Zalmon.

What's Gonna Happen

You're going to create instant snow in a new diaper.

The How Behind the Wow

In ultra diapers there is a grainy powder called sodium polyacrylate. This is a synthetic polymer which can absorb 90 times its weight of water. The powder is sprinkled into the cotton rectangle at the bottom of the diaper. As the powder absorbs liquid, it (the powder) turns into a gel. This is the same material that is used in the Disappearing Engineering demo in this book. However, this time you will actually show the powder at work.

What You Need

Luvs® Ultra Leakguard diapers
Scissors or knife
Measuring cup
Tablespoon

Plate
Glass
Water
Resealable plastic bags (optional)

What You Do

1. Open a diaper out onto the plate.
2. Use the scissors to cut around the blue rectangle in the center of the diaper, not cutting completely through the diaper. You are going to remove this rectangle from the diaper. If you begin cutting at one end, it's then easier to simply tear out the rectangle. Toss the blue rectangle away.
3. Below the rectangle is another thin layer of cotton and powder. Cut through the top of this to expose the powder beneath. At each end of this underneath rectangle, tear the cut sideways to expose as much of the powder as possible.
4. Pour a half cup to a cup of water all over the powder.
5. Wait for a minute and a half. Spoon up some of the powder, which is now in the form of soft, crystal-looking "diamonds." That's it.
6. For your presentation you'll start from scratch. Plan on doing all of the science part at the first so the diamonds can be made during your talk. The plastic bags are for giving a spoonful of the diamonds to each of the children, if you want to do this.
7. Dispose of the diaper, etc., in the trash.
8. Don't forget—have the diaper, plate, water, and scissors ready to go.

What You Say

We've got a talk and a half for you today. I call it "Diaper Diamonds." *(Show diaper.)* I'm going to start right in by cutting this blue rectangle out of the diaper. *(Do this.)* Now I'll cut down the middle of this part. We're really doing a lot of cutting on this diaper, aren't we? Okay, got that open. One last step. I'll pour water all over the middle of the diaper.

Now I'll tell you what this is all about. There's a verse in Psalm 68. It's Psalm 68:14 to be exact. The verse says this, "When the Almighty scattered the kings in the land, it was like snow fallen on Mount Zalmon."

You and I—many people, for that matter—don't usually think of snow as being in the forecast for the country of Israel. To be such a small country, however, Israel has a wide variety of weather. From the high, snowy elevations of Mt. Hermon in the north to the hotness of the desert lands in the south, Israel has long been a land of contrasts. Though Zalmon wasn't as snow covered as Mt. Hermon, it must have had snow from time to time. That's what this verse says, and if it's in the Bible, that's got to be the way it was, is, and will be.

So it is we turn our attention back to our diaper and the Diaper Diamonds we have made. That water was absorbed by a powder in the diaper. *(Scoop up a spoonful.)* And look, we've got little diamonds by the spoonful. Would you like to hold some in your hand? Tell you what I'll do. I have plastic bags here. I'll give each of you some to take with you. It's just one more reminder about the many interesting things that are brought up in the Bible. That way, when you see the Diaper Diamonds, you can remember about God making snow fall on Mt. Zalmon.

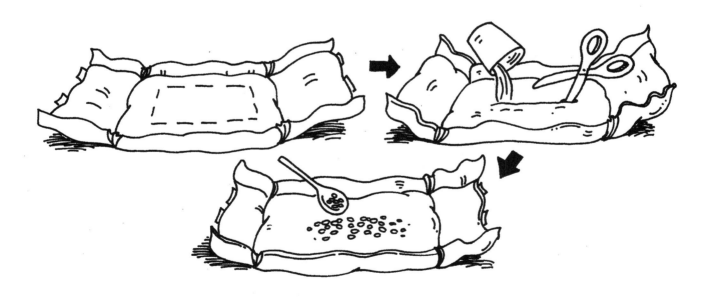

But Will It Fly?

Psalm 71:17
Since my youth, God, you have taught me, and to this day I declare your marvelous deeds.

What's Gonna Happen
You will fly a straw across the room.

The How Behind the Wow
The two paper rings, one smaller and the other larger, cause air to flow over the straw. This gives it lift and, as a result, the straw actually flies.

What You Need
Straw (regular, not flex)   Tape
Bible   3 x 5 index card
Scissors   Plain paper
Ruler   Hammer (for show only)
Sports ball (for show only)

What You Do
1. Use the scissors to cut three lengthwise strips from the index card. Each strip should be ¾ inch wide.
2. Tape one of the strips in a circle. Tape inside and out.
3. Tape the other two strips end-to-end. Tape top and bottom. Now tape this strip into a circle.
4. Tape the smaller circle to one end of the straw. The straw will be taped inside the circle. This is now the front of the "plane."
5. In the same way, tape the larger circle onto the other end of the straw. This is now the back of the plane. The circles should line up with each other. This all sounds easy but . . . I'm obviously challenged.
6. Hold the plane at shoulder height, with the circles above the straw. The front is pointed slightly upward. Toss the plane gently, but firmly forward. It should travel some 15 feet before touching down for a landing. Also try throwing the plane with the circles below the straw just for comparison. In your program, you'll use the way that works best.
7. Make a paper airplane from the plain paper. Doesn't matter if it will fly or not; it just has to look the part. You will be throwing it, so don't make a plane with a sharp point.
8. Take straw plane, paper plane, Bible, hammer, and sports ball for presentation.

What You Say

One of the very best things about God is that we can worship him at any age and stage of our life. We don't have to wait till we're old. David knew this. Listen to what he says in Psalm 71:17, "Since my youth, God, you have taught me, and to this day I declare your marvelous deeds."

You see how it worked? God taught David, then David declared that knowledge to others. When we pass along God's love, in a way we are being ministers for God. That's a thought, isn't it? That each of us in our own way can minister for God.

Check these things out. *(First, hold up Bible.)* When you see the Bible, do you think of someone who ministers? Sure, you do. The Bible and ministers go hand in hand. *(Show hammer.)* But what about a hammer? We don't usually put a hammer and ministry together, do we? They can be, though. A carpenter can minister to people. Jesus himself was a carpenter. In the same way *(show sports ball)*, a football coach or basketball player can share the love of God with others. Ministry can take many forms.

(Show two planes.) With that in mind, I have two planes. One looks like a plane. The other looks like, well, a straw with two circles taped on it. It certainly doesn't look like a plane. Let's check our paper plane first. *(Throw the paper plane. If it flies . . .)* See, our plane did okay. *(If it dies . . .)* Hmm, not so great.

Now for our circle plane. *(Toss straw plane.)* Wow, would you look at that! It went halfway across the room. It's a real plane! In the same way, you and I and all believers are ministers for God. We each can declare his marvelous deeds. It's not the sight, it's the flight that counts. *(One last toss of straw plane.)*

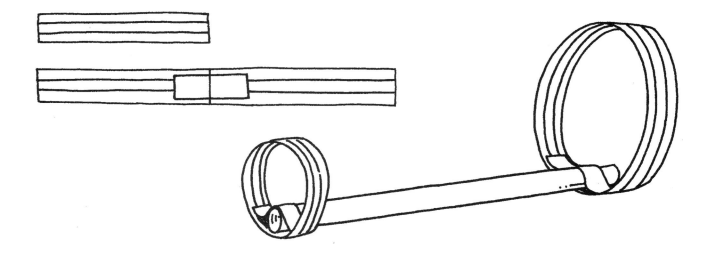

His Grip Won't Slip

Psalm 73:23
Yet I am always with you; you hold me by my right hand.

What's Gonna Happen
You will pick up a screwdriver. *Yay!* You will not pick up a screwdriver. *Boo!*

The How Behind the Wow
The end of the screwdriver is called the bit. In one instance you will lift the screwdriver by the bit. No problem; plenty of friction between your fingers and the bit. Then you will dip the bit in dishwashing liquid and try to lift the screwdriver. Friction is reduced to the point that it is nearly impossible to lift the screwdriver.

What You Need
Small, clear, plastic cup

Dishwashing liquid

Newspaper

Screwdrivers (at least 3; regular, not Phillips)

Cleanup materials (water, paper towels)

What You Do
1. Lay down some newspaper, several sheets thick.
2. Pour an inch of dishwashing liquid into the plastic cup.
3. Lift a screwdriver by the bit. Easy.
4. Now dip the bit of the screwdriver into the dishwashing soap. Try to grip and lift the screwdriver by the bit again. Do this above the newspaper. The "nearly" is in "The How Behind the Wow" because someone out there is going to have an amazing grip. For most of us, however, there is not enough friction to grip the bit. This includes the children to whom you will be speaking. The "slip" overrides the "grip."
5. Clean the screwdriver. Have all materials (including ones for cleanup) with you for your talk. The two extra screwdrivers are for volunteers. You can certainly add more screwdrivers for this demo, as well as other non-sharp tools and/or kitchen utensils.

What You Say

One of the best feelings in the world is knowing there is a path we are to travel throughout life. God has a plan for each of us. He's given us all different abilities and talents. He is willing to lead, guide, and direct us if we are willing to be led. I hope that you will begin to trust God's leading at a young age and walk with him all your days.

A verse that helps me understand God's leading is Psalm 73:23. It says, "Yet I am always with you; you hold me by my right hand." God holds us by our hand. Isn't that a great thought?

Today I have something to remind me of God's grip on our hand. It's this screwdriver. Watch when I pick it up by the end. *(Do this.)* See what a good grip I have. Even though I'm just pinching it with my two fingers, my index and thumb, I've got the screwdriver in my grip. My grip on the screwdriver is like God's grip on our hand. We're his and he's ours.

Now I'll spread out a little newspaper because I'm going to dip the end of the screwdriver into this dishwashing liquid and try to grip it. *(Do this.)* Whoa, that slipped right out of my hand. And I was trying my best. That reminds me that we don't want to be led by just anyone or anything. You may like TV, but don't plan on TV leading your life. You may love sports, but don't let sports be the thing that leads your life. It's the same with video games, classmates, movies, and on and on. Only God has a grip and a path for you that will be the very best way to go.

Okay, I've got two more screwdrivers. Would two of you like to try the grip test? *(After they are done, clean up.)* So there you have it, my young friends. Psalm 73:23 says it best, "Yet I am always with you; you hold me by my right hand." God is always with us to lead and guide us. And that is something we can always get a grip on—whether you are right handed or left.

Near and Dear

Psalm 73:28
But as for me, it is good to be near God.

What's Gonna Happen
You will set a quarter on a coat hanger, take a deep breath, then spin the coat hanger. The quarter will stay on for the ride.

The How Behind the Wow
Centripetal force is an inner pull on objects going in a circle. Centrifugal force is the outward-pulling tug you and I feel when going around a corner. As you spin the coat hanger, that same centrifugal force pushes the quarter outward against the hanger. Therefore, the quarter stays put. As with anything, the hardest part is the dismount.

What You Need
Plastic coat hanger
Sandpaper
Quarter

What You Do
1. Oftentimes plastic coat hangers have upraised ridges on the crossbar. Since this is where you're going to place the quarter, those tiny ridges aren't good things. Use the sandpaper to sand across the center top of the crossbar. You don't have to make it perfectly smooth, but a little leveling is a good thing.
2. Hang the hook of the coat hanger over your index finger.
3. With your other hand, place the quarter on the hanger.
4. Gently ease into this, swinging lightly back and forth. After a bit, just go for it. Swing the coat hanger in a full circle and keep spinning. This doesn't have to be ultrafast, just a nice steady pace.
5. When you're ready to stop, ease off the swinging. On the last rotation, step with the swing and *give* a little with it. Often—not always, but often—the quarter will remain on the coat hanger as you stop. That's a perfect 10.
6. Another dismount is to flip the coat hanger into the air. As things come down, catch the quarter in one hand and the coat hanger in the other. Good luck with that!
7. In your presentation, be sure to stand so that no one is on either side of the coat hanger. Don't want anyone to accidentally get hit by a flying quarter.

What You Say

One of my very favorite verses in the book of Psalms is Psalm 73:28. It's an easy verse to remember. In fact, maybe we should try to memorize it. What do you think? Want to give it a try? Great. Here's the verse, "But as for me, it is good to be near God." Isn't that a neat thought? Let's say it together. "But as for me, it is good to be near God." Do you have it? Let's try it again. "But as for me, it is good to be near God."

The thing is, it really is good to be near God. I can't think of anywhere else I'd rather be, can you? Think of all you have. You've got your parents, your grandparents, and your friends, not to mention your church family. Along with all these people, there is God. Wow, we are blessed. It truly is good to be near God.

It feels so good to be near God that I'm reminded of this coat hanger and this quarter. *(Show.)* The coat hanger represents God; the quarter represents us. *(Spread your arms out wide with the coat hanger in one hand, the quarter in the other.)* This is the way we would be if we weren't near God. We would be miles apart. Who would want that? Not us, that's for sure. Instead, here we are near God. *(Put quarter on hanger.)*

Okay, now check this out. I've practiced for this, so we've got to give it a try. Being near God is a very exciting way to live. *(Begin gently swinging hanger back and forth.)* Fact is, we soon come to the conclusion that there is no better way to ride through this life, and here we go. *(Swing hanger and quarter in a full circle.)* It is good being near God. This is the best way to live. And now, we ease down and come to a stop. *(Do this.)*

Whoa, that was fun. So let's always remember— and live by—Psalm 73:28, "But as for me, it is good to be near God."

SAND

Banana Hamma

Psalm 78:9, 10
The men of Ephraim, though armed with bows, turned back on the day of battle; they did not keep God's covenant and refused to live by his law.

What's Gonna Happen
You will use a banana to hammer a nail into a board.

The How Behind the Wow
To do this demo, you need to freeze the banana. Put a large, fresh banana in your freezer. It freezes big time. Even that isn't enough though, without the right kind of sharp object. This should be something with a lot of surface area on the head. A giant pushpin is perfect. A roofing nail will work in a pinch. Between the frozen-solid banana and the proper sharp object, you will have a hit on your hands.

What You Need
Fresh large banana
Wood board
Ice

Giant-size pushpin or roofing nail
Cooler
Hammer

What You Do
1. Put the large banana in your freezer for at least six hours.
2. Take the banana from the freezer. Use it to hammer the giant pushpin or nail into the board.
3. Okay, you're good to go. Remove the pin. Take all materials with you for your talk. The cooler and ice are to keep the banana frozen as you transfer it from your freezer to the place where you'll do your talk. Put ice all around the banana. The sooner you can do your talk, the better.
4. Don't forget to take the hammer with you.

What You Say

Have you ever heard of Plan B? Plan B is a backup to the main plan. Let's say you're going to walk two blocks to your grandmother's house. That's Plan A. But when it's time for you to walk and it's raining like crazy outside, Plan B might be for your mom to drive you. See how Plan B works? It's a backup plan.

I wonder if God has had to have Plan Bs throughout history too. Check this out. Psalm 78:9, 10 says, "The men of Ephraim, though armed with bows, turned back on the day of battle; they did not keep God's covenant and refused to live by his law." These soldiers had everything they needed. However, when crunch time came they wouldn't step up for God. So God had to go to Plan B and find others who would go into battle for him.

With all that said, I have this hammer. *(Show hammer.)* I want to use the hammer to drive this giant pushpin *(show pushpin)* into this board. That's a pretty simple job for a hammer, right? But suppose that hammer woke up this morning on the wrong side of the toolbox. You look at the hammer *(do this)* and can tell by its expression that something's not right. So you go, "Mr. Hammer, you feeling alright? Are you ready to get the job done today?"

That ol' hammer says, "Nope." *(Shake hammer head sideways.)* "I'm just not up to hammering today. I've got a headache."

Now what do you say to that? Who ever heard of a hammer having a headache? Only one thing to do. Go to Plan B, right? Fortunately I just happen to have Plan B in this cooler. *(Take out frozen banana and show your audience.)* How about that, kids? A frozen banana without a headache. Here, I'll show you. *(Drive in the pushpin with the banana. When finished, show the board with the pin to everyone.)* And there you have it, my young friends. We used a banana hamma.

Question is, what can we take from today's talk? Just this. When God wants to use us for his glory, let's be sure and answer the call. Okay? Let's not make God have to go to Plan B. When it comes to driving in sharp objects, frozen bananas are okay. But hammers are the real deal. Let's you and I be the real deal for God.

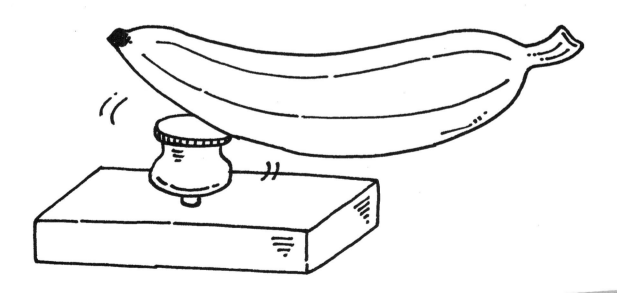

Lettuce Be Strong

Psalm 78:10
They did not keep God's covenant and refused to live by his law.

What's Gonna Happen
You will soak a lettuce leaf in salt water. The lettuce leaf will lose its zip, zing, and every other thing.

The How Behind the Wow
Osmosis is the passage of water through a membrane. The osmosis occurs from the higher water concentration side of the membrane to the lower. There are membranes surrounding plant and animal cells. If salt water is outside of the cells, the concentration of straight-up water is higher inside the cells. Therefore, water moves out of the cells toward the salt water. Which is why, if we drink salt water, we are toast. Limp toast, but toast.

What You Need
Water

Salt

Spoon

2 large bowls (mixing bowl, baking dish, etc.)

Lettuce leaves

Ice

What You Do
1. Put several inches of water in each bowl.
2. Into one of the bowls, stir five teaspoons of salt.
3. Submerge a crisp lettuce leaf into the water of each bowl.
4. Wait for two minutes. Remove the leaves and hold them so that they stand up vertically. The fresh water leaf will stand. The salt water leaf will droop over.
5. You'll need to have the lettuce chilled on ice for your talk.
6. Have water in the bowls to begin. Plan on preparing the salt and leaves in the presence of the children at the beginning of your presentation. By the time you finish your talk, the leaves will be done.

What You Say

I'm going to start today's demo right now. As you can see, I've got these two bowls. Each bowl has water in it. I'll leave one bowl as it is. Into this other bowl, though, I'm going to pour in some salt and stir it. Last, I've got two crisp lettuce leaves. I'll put one leaf into each bowl, and we'll leave them there for a minute or two. Get it? We'll leave the leaves.

While the leaves are soaking, let me share a thought with you. That thought is this—some of the psalms from the book of Psalms are little history lessons. They look back to the many journeys of the Hebrews, recalling the ways that God led his people. Thing is, the people didn't always live the way God wanted them to. As it says in Psalm 78:10, "They did not keep God's covenant and refused to live by his law." That's an oops if I ever heard one.

Wonder why they behaved like that? That's kind of a mystery, isn't it? They would obey for a while, then they'd run out of enthusiasm, or steam, or obedience, or something. The Bible says they were a "stiff-necked people." *Stiff-necked* means stubborn. Then, after they were stiff-necked and stubborn, their faith just drooped, sagged, and fell off of the charts. It might take as long as a whole other generation of people before they got back on track.

The main thing for us to get from this is that we don't want to repeat mistakes that others made. Still today, if we're not careful, we'll run out of steam or enthusiasm. And that's not right. God is much too important for us not to be way joyous and enthusiastic. *(Expand this thought if you think your lettuce leaves need a bit more time.)*

All of which brings us back to our lettuce. In bowl one, the unsalted bowl, I have the Israelites when they were behaving and being obedient. *(Hold up fresh leaf.)* And in bowl two, I have the Israelites when they were going through one of their disobedient spells. *(Hold up limp leaf.)* See what I mean? Their faith just was not there. And God was not happy.

Let's use the Israelites' lives as a compass. Where they went one way, let us—get it? "Lettuce" *(hold up fresh leaf)*—go the other. We will be all the stronger for it.

SALT X5

Slo-Mo Flow

Psalm 78:15, 16

He split the rocks in the wilderness and gave them water as abundant as the seas; he brought streams out of a rocky crag and made water flow down like rivers.

What's Gonna Happen

You'll pour four liquids down a slanted surface, checking them for speed. Resistance to flow is termed *viscosity*. Liquids that flow slowly are said to have high viscosity.

What You Need

Drinking glass with water
Several books
Spoons
Stopwatch (optional)
Food coloring

Metal baking pan, glass dish, or pane of glass
Liquids for testing (ketchup, chocolate syrup, motor oil, water)
Flat pan for catching the liquids

What You Do

1. Stack three or four books on a table.
2. Turn the baking pan upside down. (I use the glass from an inexpensive picture frame.) Rest one end on the books, other end inside the catch pan.
3. Put a spoonful of each liquid onto the top of the pan or pane. Use a separate spoon per liquid. Make sure there is enough space between the liquids so they don't mix on the way down. Place the spoons in the glass of water as you use them. Be sure to put the ketchup on first. With the others, the order doesn't matter.
4. The food coloring is for the water to help it show up better.
5. Check a clock when you start the ketchup. Time the flow of the other liquids with a watch or stopwatch. Or, if you prefer, just observe.
6. When finished, you're done. Clean up; have things set up and ready to go for your talk. By the way, the ketchup takes forever. If you wait for it to finish, this could be a 20-minute talk.

What You Say

The thing about the language in the book of Psalms is that it oftentimes paints a picture. Language that does that is said to be picturesque. Paints a picture—picturesque. Get it? Sure, you do. Take, for example, today's verses. Psalm 78:15, 16 says, "He split the rocks in the wilderness and gave them water as abundant as the seas; he brought streams out of a rocky crag and made water flow down like rivers."

The Israelites were in the desert, and they were hot and thirsty. To give them water, God broke the rocks. Streams just poured out. What a picture! It's picturesque, right? No doubt.

In honor of the streams pouring down, I've got this pan slanted against these books. I'm going to pour a spoonful of four liquids onto the pan. *(Show liquids.)* The liquids are motor oil, chocolate syrup, ketchup, and water. We're going to see which "stream in the desert" goes slowest. Which do you think will be the slowest liquid? Which do you think will be the fastest? *(Encourage answers.)* Only one way to find out, right? So here we go. Ketchup first. *(Pour on liquids.)*

(As they ooze or zoom down the surface . . .) Looks like the ketchup will definitely be the slowest. Who picked that one? Good for you. But you know, whether slow or fast, they remind us of those verses: God "split the rocks in the wilderness and gave them water as abundant as the seas; he brought streams out of a rocky crag and made water flow down like rivers." And those streams in the desert were pure water for the people to drink. They were happy.

With that, I think we'll just call it a day. The ketchup is on its own.

It's Raining Grain

Psalm 78:24, 25

He rained down manna for the people to eat, he gave them the grain of heaven. Human beings ate the bread of angels; he sent them all the food they could eat.

What's Gonna Happen

You'll make a paper helicopter then drop the copter.

The How Behind the Wow

The blades of your helicopter give it stability, or rotational inertia. The copter always falls straight downward to the target.

What You Need

2 sheets of plain paper
Transparent tape
Ruler

Scissors
Paper clip (small)
Pen

What You Do

1. Use the ruler to measure a two-inch section across a sheet of paper. Line this off and cut with scissors. This will give you a strip of paper that is 2" x 8 ½" long. Make two of these strips. Leave one of them flat, just as is. You will use this briefly during your talk.
2. With the other strip, starting at one end make a ¼ inch fold upward. Continue folding up five more times—six folds total. Hold this in place with a paper clip. This will be the bottom of your copter.
3. At the other end, use the ruler and pen to make a 2½" line down the center.
4. With the scissors, cut on the line. These are your blades. Fold one blade in a 90-degree angle in one direction. Fold the other blade at a 90-degree angle in the opposite direction.
5. In the open space between the blades and the paper clip, use your pen to write "grain" on one side. Draw bread (loaf, slice, roll, biscuit, etc.) on the other.
6. Check out your copter. Standing on a chair, drop it from head height. I like to write "Camp" on a sheet of paper and place that on the floor. That gives me a target to land on in the Israelite camp.
7. You're set. Take this copter with you for your talk. Don't forget the extra flat strip.

What You Say

The book of Psalms is basically right in the middle of the Bible, in more ways than one. Sometimes you can read a verse in the Psalms and that verse will shoot you straight toward the New Testament. Other times, a verse will take you back to the older days of the Old Testament. Do you see? Psalms is in the middle for going forward or backward.

That's the case with today's verses, Psalm 78:24, 25. "He rained down manna for the people to eat, he gave them the grain of heaven. Human beings ate the bread of angels; he sent them all the food they could eat." This took place during the time the Israelites left Egypt, heading for the promised land of Canaan. Out in the desert they needed food. Each day God would send down nice little bread bites for the people to eat. It was called manna, and it always came down at the right time and in the right place. That's the way God was—and is—with his blessings. On time and on target.

It reminds me of this copter. *(Show strip of flat paper only.)* Does that look like a little copter to you? I agree. It doesn't to me either. Maybe that's what the people thought when they heard about bread coming their way. They'd look up at the sky and go, "Bread out of the sky? I don't think so." But God thought so. That's what mattered.

So what about this copter? *(Show copter.)* Look, it has *grain* written on one side and a picture of bread on the other. I'll just put the "Israelite camp" on the floor *(place plain sheet of paper on floor)* and stand in this chair. Let's see if the grain comes anywhere close to the camp, shall we? Here we go. . . . Copter #1. *(Drop away.)* How about that shot? Pretty good, huh?

I think it deserves another; see if we can go two for two. *(Have someone hand it up to you.)* Copter #2, coming down. *(Drop.)* And there you are, kids—on time and on target. Perfect. Isn't that just like God?

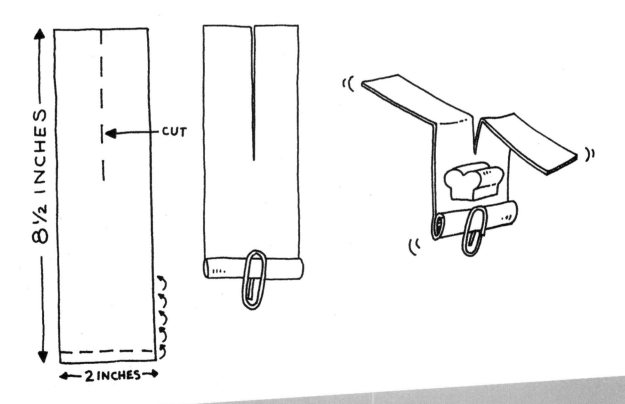

8½ INCHES

CUT

2 INCHES

Penny for Your Thoughts

Psalm 78:70, 71
He chose David his servant and took him from the sheep pens; from tending the sheep he brought him to be the shepherd of his people Jacob, of Israel his inheritance.

What's Gonna Happen
You're going to file around the edge of a penny.

The How Behind the Wow
During 1982 pennies went from being all copper to mostly zinc. Since 1983 the only copper has been an extremely thin copper foil on the surface. When filing around the circumference of a penny that is dated from 1983 on, you will see a shiny, silvery interior of zinc rather than copper.

What You Need
New pennies from 1983 until present
File

What You Do
1. File around the edge of a new penny till you've removed all the copper coating. That's it. You're looking at zinc.
2. The extra pennies are for the children. If your group is small enough, you may want to file a penny for each of them.
3. Take the file with you for your talk.

What You Say

From the time he was a boy, David had amazing skills. Just check out some of the things at which he was good. He could play musical instruments, sling a rock with perfect accuracy, fight wild animals, sing with a great voice, and write beautiful poetry. Wow. That's quite a list, isn't it? Aren't you impressed?

I'll tell you what. God was impressed. It's no wonder we read these words in Psalm 78:70, 71: "He [God] chose David his servant and took him from the sheep pens; from tending the sheep he brought him to be the shepherd of his people Jacob, of Israel his inheritance." David went from guiding sheep to guiding a nation.

One thing about David impressed God above all others. Do you know what that was? *(Accept all answers.)* We can find the answer in the book of 1 Samuel, chapter 16. In that chapter Samuel was sent to anoint one of Jesse's sons as the new king of Israel. Thing is, Samuel wasn't sure which of Jesse's sons to anoint. And Jesse had eight boys. God told Samuel, "Don't worry, I'll show you which one. Man looks at the outward appearance, but the Lord looks at the heart."

And y'all, that's what God liked best about David—his heart. David had a heart for God. Brings to mind this penny. *(Show penny, but not sides where you've filed.)* Does anybody know what pennies are made of? *(Accept all answers.)* Sure, that's right. Copper. Does everybody agree? Me too.

But you know what? We'd all be wrong. That's true. Since 1983 pennies have been made of zinc. The only copper is a thin copper foil layer on the outside of the zinc. Here, I'll show you. *(Show sides of penny.)* See that shiny silver color? That's zinc. It's a different metal from copper. But you can't see the zinc unless you have one of these. *(Show file.)*

And so it was with David. Anyone might have thought David's heart was such that he only cared about himself. But no. David cared about the things of God. In short, David had a heart for God, which is why Samuel anointed him to be the next king of Israel.

Having a heart for God is the goal for each of us, my friends. The world may see what's on the outside, just like this copper. But you and I know it's the inside that counts. That's how we want to live *(show zinc one last time),* having a heart for God.

(Optional . . .) I just happen to have a "heart for God" souvenir for each of you today.

Fun and Done

Psalm 84:10b
I would rather be a doorkeeper in the house of my God than dwell in the tents of the wicked.

What's Gonna Happen
You'll light birthday candles in a pie pan, then put them out with a dry ice fog.

The How Behind the Wow
Dry ice is frozen carbon dioxide gas. When dry ice thaws (sublimates), the ice goes directly back to the gaseous state. It bypasses the liquid phase so that there are no drops (thus its name, dry ice). Carbon dioxide gas is heavier than air. Therefore, it sinks. Also, since carbon dioxide gas doesn't support burning, it extinguishes the flames of the birthday candles.

What You Need
Clay

Matches

Water

5 birthday candles

Pitcher

CD player and CD (optional)

Dry ice (available at some grocery stores)

2 pie pans

Measuring cups

Hammer

Tongs

What You Do
1. Arrange four small mounds of clay (any pattern) in one pie pan. Stand a birthday candle in each ball of clay. In the second pie pan, put a mound of clay in the center. Stand one candle there.
2. Break the dry ice with the hammer. (Note: Purchase a block of dry ice at a grocery store. Preferably buy this the day of your talk; no sooner than the day before. The dry ice will be in a plastic bag. Pick it up by this bag. **Never touch the actual dry ice.** Put the block of dry ice in a paper grocery sack, set it into your cooler, and put the lid on.)
3. Use the tongs to set three or four pieces of dry ice into the pitcher.
4. Pie pans should be two feet apart. Light the candles in both pans.
5. Put warm water into the pitcher with the dry ice. Two cups of water should be plenty. Vapors will flow out and down from the pitcher.
6. Pour vapors from the pitcher onto the four candles. Don't pour any of the water out. The vapors are actually water vapor that is being cooled and condensed in the air. There is plenty of carbon dioxide gas within the vapors, however. This CO_2 gas will put out the candles. Allow the single candle in the second pan to remain burning.

7. Start from scratch in your talk. Maybe fresh candles. Just before your talk, you can go ahead and put the dry ice into the pitcher. Remember, dry ice only lasts two or three days in the cooler (don't store it in your refrigerator freezer), so you'll want to purchase it very near to the time for your presentation.

What You Say

One of the neatest verses in the book of Psalms is found in Psalm 84. That psalm is written by the Sons of Korah. In Psalm 84:10 they say, "I would rather be a doorkeeper in the house of my God than dwell in the tents of the wicked." Being a doorkeeper is a reminder that God wants each of us to have the heart of a servant, to always be on the lookout for ways we can do things for other people. When we are doing for others, we are doing for God.

So with that in mind, here I have two pie pans and some candles. Over here is the lone doorkeeper, while in the other pan is the party crowd. I'll just light the candles and the night has begun. The doorkeeper is just quietly going about his or her business. Meanwhile, over here the night is just beginning. They are laughing, joking, singing *(if you want to play some music from a CD, that would work),* just having a big ol' time.

Around midnight word circulates that the smoke show is coming. Word shoots through the crowd. "The smoke show is coming! The smoke show is coming!" Sure enough, here it comes. *(Pour warm water onto the dry ice. As vapors flow . . .)* "Hooray!" they all shout. "We've been needing some new excitement. Bring on the smoke show!"

(Pour CO_2 gas over the four candles, putting out the flames. As the last one goes out, set down the pitcher and pick up the other pie pan.) There is a lot to be said about being a doorkeeper for the Lord. Not the least of which is that our flame burns brightest when we are focused on doing for God.

POUR VAPORS
ONLY

Meet in the Middle

Psalm 86:15
But you, Lord, are a compassionate and gracious God, slow to anger, abounding in love and faithfulness.

What's Gonna Happen
You will balance a yardstick horizontally on your two index fingers, then slide your fingers toward each other. The key is to start with your fingers at different lengths from each end of the yardstick (maybe one finger at the 6-inch mark, the other at 24 inches). It looks as if they would meet midway between the two starting points (which would be at the 15-inch site) but, no. Never happens. They always meet in the middle of the yardstick.

The How Behind the Wow
As you slide your fingers toward each other, the finger nearest the center doesn't slide. This is because the weight of the yardstick rests on that finger. As you keep sliding your finger(s) toward the center, the weight shifts back and forth till the end result is that your two fingers always meet in the middle of the yardstick.

What You Need
Yardstick
Pen or pencil

What You Do
1. The center of the yardstick should be at 18 inches. Because of imperfections in the wood, however, the gravitational center may be slightly different. Balance the yardstick on your finger to find its center. Mark this location with your pen or pencil.
2. Rest the yardstick on your two index fingers. Let's use the distances you will use in your talk. Put one finger at 10 inches, the other at 34.
3. Try to slide your fingers toward each other. The only finger that will move is the one farther from the center. Eventually, it will get close enough to the center so that the weight of the stick shifts. Continue sliding both fingers till they end up in the middle of the yardstick. The stick stays balanced the whole time. Does it this way every time.

What You Say

Our God, boys and girls, is an awesome God. That's really true, not just words to say. His love is steady, even if ours isn't. His faithfulness is perfect, every day in every way. We are his children and he wants the best for each of us. God truly is awesome.

Psalm 86:15 reminds us of this. That verse says, "But you, Lord, are a compassionate and gracious God, slow to anger, abounding in love and faithfulness."

In a way God reminds me of this yardstick. I'll show you what I mean. I'll put one index finger out on this end at the 34-inch mark. That represents us. And I'll put my other index finger at the 10-inch mark. We'll let that represent God. Notice that my fingers aren't the same distance from the middle of the stick. Question is: If I slide my fingers toward each other, will they meet in the middle of my fingers *(point out 22-inch location)* or will they meet in the middle of the yardstick *(point out pen mark location)*? *(Accept all answers and thoughts.)*

Good thinking. Only way I know to find out is to give things a try, so here we go. *(Slide fingers toward each other.)* Hey, check it out. Our end is the only one that's moving. That's because more of the stick is resting on God's end. But watch, as my finger gets closer to the middle, now God's end begins moving. Now both ends, and look. They meet right in the middle of the yardstick. It's really cool. And it works like that every time.

It reminds me that God is loving and faithful. When we come toward him he is always willing to meet us in the middle. He doesn't just stay way over on his side, not caring or feeling for us. No way. God loves us and is always coming our direction. Isn't that a great thing?

So that you'll know I wasn't just making my fingers meet in the middle, would one of you like to try the yardstick test? Great. All you do is put your fingers at two different distances from the center and away you go. Or, I should say, away you slide to meet in the middle with God.

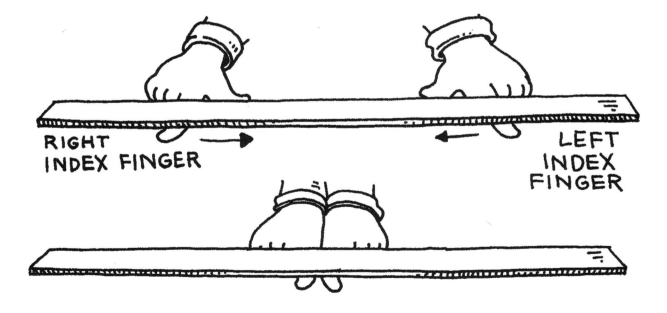

RIGHT INDEX FINGER

LEFT INDEX FINGER

Where Did the Song Go Wrong?

Psalm 88:13b
In the morning my prayer comes before you.

What's Gonna Happen
You're going to construct some racket-makers for the kids.

The How Behind the Wow
Music is a blend of sounds that come together harmoniously. This blend of sounds is pleasing to the listener. On the other hand, noise and racket are random sounds colliding and interfering with each other. Must be true; I've made the latter two all my life.

What You Need
2 empty tin cans   Birthday whizzers or horns (gotta have sound)
Rocks   Bicycle horn
Metal spoons   Dried rice
Metal bowl   Plastic bottle with cap
Duct tape   Bible
Busted guitar (optional)

What You Do
1. Pour an inch of dried rice in the plastic bottle. Put on cap.
2. The two cans should be empty with just the top ends open. Put 8–10 small to medium-size rocks in one of the cans. Put the other can end-to-end with the "rock" can. Both open ends should be facing each other. Use duct tape to tape the two cans closed.
3. The rest of "What You Do" is just getting things. You are going to create one of the noisiest bands anyone's ever heard:
   a. one child with the plastic bottle and rice
   b. one child with the tin cans and rocks
   c. one child with metal spoons on a metal bowl
   d. one child with the bicycle horn (optional at this point)
   e. any number with the birthday horns and whizzers; your call
   f. at this point you may as well throw in a busted guitar
4. Bookmark Psalm 42 to have a child try to read silently.

What You Say

One of the best times of the day is the morning. Things are quiet then; you can have a little time to yourself. The morning is especially good for spending time with God. Some people do this every day. They call it having a quiet time. A quiet time is an excellent thing. In Psalm 42:2 the writer asks, "When can I go and meet with God?" That question is answered in Psalm 88:13, "In the morning my prayer comes before you."

Let's see how a quiet time can work. I need volunteers all over the place:

One of you will take this Bible bookmarked at Psalm 42.

Another, this water bottle with rice in it.

One, these cans of rocks.

Here are a couple of birthday whizzers and horns.

And I need someone to bang on the bottom of this metal bowl.

(Anything else is up to you.)

Okay, everybody with a noisemaker keep your eyes on me. When I point to you, start shaking, banging, and booming with your instrument.

Before that, though, we'll have our first volunteer read the Bible to herself—Psalm 42 to be exact. Remember that is the psalm that asked, "When can I go and meet with God?" And one good answer is morning. So here we go; it's morning time. Let's all be *real* quiet, so she can have a quiet time. *Shhh. (Whisper . . .)* Way to go. You're doing great.

(Just as the child has had time to read maybe two verses, say . . .) Whoa, must have gotten a late start today. Things are stirring in the house. *(Point to the plastic bottle of rice.)* I can hear people moving around. But you keep reading. Now there's racket in the kitchen. *(Point to the can of rocks.)* And out on the street there is traffic everywhere. *(Point to the birthday whizzers and horns.)* Keep reading. Oh, my goodness, they're fighting over the bathroom. *(Point to the metal bowl and spoons.)* How's your quiet time coming along? *(Accept reader's response.)* Are you getting the point of Psalm 42?

(Quiet everyone down.) No, not really. 'Cause a quiet time is meant to be quiet. Kids, when can you go and meet with God? The writer of Psalm 88 says you can meet with God first thing in the morning *(point to all the noisemakers)* **before** your day kicks into ultrahigh gear. *(Start the noise again, then shout above the racket.)* Check out having a quiet time. You'll love it.

TIN CANS

DUCT TAPE

ROCKS

Deep and Wide

Psalm 92:5
How great are your works, LORD, how profound your thoughts!

What's Gonna Happen
You're going to pour some colored water from beneath a layer of oil.

The How Behind the Wow
Liquids have density, just as solids do. As you likely know, water is denser than oil. And, since they don't mix, they form layers with oil always on top. You're going to make a way to pour the water from beneath the oil.

What You Need
Water	Gallon milk jug (plastic, clean, with cap)
Food coloring	Scissors
Cooking oil	Ruler
Permanent marker	Glass

What You Do
1. Use the ruler to measure down 4½ inches from the top of the milk jug.
2. Mark this distance with the marker.
3. With the scissors, cut all the way around the jug. Be sure to cut straight through the handle.
4. Put the cap on the jug and turn upside down. Set on table. Be sure you have some way to keep the top-heavy container from tipping over.
5. Put 8–10 drops of food coloring in the jug, then fill halfway with water.
6. Tilt the container a bit and gently pour in cooking oil to a depth of half an inch.
7. Pour the colored water out through the handle into the glass. You will basically be able to get all of the water out, while leaving all of the oil behind.
8. Clean everything up and you're ready to go. Plan on starting with all fresh liquids for your talk so you can begin at step 7.

What You Say

We're talking today about the deep end of the Christian pool. You see, the deeper things of God require our time and attention. *(Use your hand in the air here to make layers.)* We can know God on the surface *(hand above your head)*; or we can read his Word and know him deeper *(hand in front of face)*; or we can really study and pray and know him deeply *(hand in front of chest)*. You and I want to always go for the depth.

I'll show you what I mean. Here I have a milk jug, or what's left of one. It's just the top, but it's turned upside down so it's a pitcher. The handle of the bottle is our spout. In the milk jug I have some colored water on the bottom. Then on top I have a layer of cooking oil. The colored water represents the deep things of God—those things that we want to learn about God and experience with him. As Psalm 92:5 says, "How great are your works, LORD, how profound your thoughts!" The *King James Version* says, "Thy thoughts are very deep."

Getting to those great works and deep thoughts is the key. Prayer is one huge means; Bible study is another. It takes time to go deep. But when we do, we'll start connecting with God on a whole other level, a deeper level. He starts sharing his heart with us, which is what I'll show here by pouring out the good, deep water, and leaving the oil behind. *(Pour water from handle into the glass.)*

See what I mean? *(Hold up glass.)* Our time spent with God wasn't wasted by any stretch. In return for our time and effort, he's giving us of his very best. I'd say that's a good exchange *(hold up both containers)* no matter how you look at it.

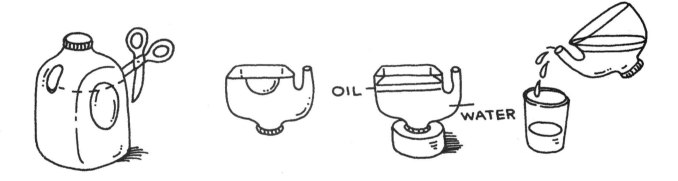

Don't Mope over the Soap

Psalm 95:7b, 8a
Today, if only you would hear his voice, "Do not harden your hearts as you did at Meribah."

What's Gonna Happen
You're going to make up a batch of hard water, then test it with dishwashing liquid.

The How Behind the Wow
Hard water is caused by an excess of minerals, particularly calcium and magnesium. These minerals react with soap, making it difficult to form lather or bubbles. Soft water has very little, if any, calcium and magnesium.

What You Need
2–2-liter soda pop bottles   Dishwashing liquid
Scissors   Paper plate
Epsom salt   Distilled water
8 oz. Styrofoam™ cup   2 plastic spoons

What You Do
1. First, take the labels off of the bottles. Do this by cutting through the labels with the scissors. While running hot tap water over the glued area, gently pull the label away from the bottle.
2. Fill the foam cup with distilled water. Pour this into the first two-liter bottle. We'll call this Bottle A.
3. Pour a spoonful of dishwashing liquid into Bottle A. Twist on the cap. Don't shake at this point. That will come later.
4. Pour a cupful of distilled water into Bottle B. Add a spoonful of Epsom salt. If some of the salt misses Bottle B as you pour, you might curl a small piece of paper to make a "salt slide" (funnel). Twist on the cap and shake well to dissolve the salt.
5. Now, add a spoonful of dishwashing liquid and re-cap the bottle. Shake the two bottles at the same time for approximately 10 seconds. Compare. There should be noticeably less suds in Bottle B. Epsom salt is chemically named magnesium sulfate, so it's high in magnesium. For a more dramatic difference, put in two spoons of Epsom salt.
6. Clean up everything well.
7. Plan on starting your demo with the distilled water in the soda pop bottles.

What You Say

Our verses today are Psalm 95:7, 8. They say, "Today, if only you would hear his voice, 'Do not harden your hearts as you did at Meribah.'" What these verses are talking about is the time Moses led the Israelites out of slavery in Egypt. God told them, "Trust in me and I'll get you to the promised land." So the people trusted.

Things were good till the Israelites got out in the desert with no water, Gatorade, soda pop, or Kool Aid. That's when their trust ran thin. They started hammering away at Moses. If you ever want to read this little story, you can find it in Exodus, chapter 17. At any rate, God ended up telling Moses to hit a rock with his shepherd's staff. So, of course, Moses did it. He whacked that big ol' rock and water gushed out six ways from Sunday. Everybody was happy—except God. He always remembered how the people hadn't trusted; how they hardened their hearts in the desert at a place that came to be known as Meribah.

Hardening their hearts toward God then wasn't a good thing to do. Nor is it a good thing to do now. Here, I'll show you what I mean. In each of these soda bottles I have a cup of distilled water. Distilled water is soft water because it is low in minerals.

Into the first bottle I'll put a spoonful of liquid soap, then set my spoon on this plate. *(Do each step as you talk.)* Now I'll just cap that one and set it aside. Next, I'll use this clean spoon to drop a spoonful or two of Epsom salt into the second bottle. Epsom salt makes water hard because of the mineral magnesium. I'll cap and shake this bottle well. Now I'll add a spoonful of soap to this bottle.

Okay, there are our two bottles. And, here we go, shaking them both up. *(Shake for 10 seconds. As things settle back down in the bottles . . .)* Would you look at that? The hard water doesn't have nearly as many suds as the other bottle. Who would have thought that?

In the same way, people—even Christians—who say to God, "I'll give you this much and no more," are hardening their hearts to God and his love. Let's you and I always have a heart that is soft toward God; a heart that trusts our heavenly Father. If we do, he will fill us up with the best life we can imagine.

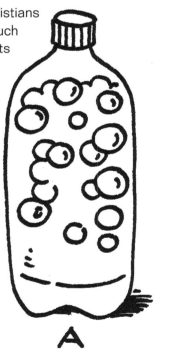
A

B

Zingy Thingy

Psalm 96:11, 12

Let the heavens rejoice, let the earth be glad; let the sea resound, and all that is in it. Let the fields be jubilant, and everything in them; let all the trees of the forest sing for joy.

What's Gonna Happen

You will use a milk jug as an amplifier of sound.

The How Behind the Wow

The sound you make will result from vibrating a metal Slinky. It gives kind of a springy sound. Using the milk jug as both an amplifier and echo chamber makes something that sounds like a Star Wars sound track. The *spring* becomes a *zing*.

What You Need

Empty, clean milk jug
Slinky® (metal)
Duct tape

X-ACTO® knife
Scissors

What You Do

1. Use the knife or scissors to cut the bottom off of the gallon milk jug. Make the cut around the jug some two inches up from the bottom. Some plastic milk jugs have a perfect line for this.
2. Use the knife to cut a small slit in the neck of the milk jug. This only has to be wide and long enough for the end of the Slinky to fit in. Make this cut just below the threads at the top.
3. Insert one end of the Slinky into the small cut. Push the Slinky in about an inch. Put tiny pieces of duct tape where the Slinky enters the bottle. This will help hold the Slinky in place.
4. With one hand, hold the open end of the milk jug to your ear. While holding the milk jug to your ear, hold the far end of the Slinky in your other hand. Use this hand to vibrate the Slinky in various ways (up, down, back, forth). You'll hear Star Wars-type sounds in the milk jug. Experiment, but go easy. The high-pitched sounds may add up on the painful side.
5. In your talk you'll have one or more of the kids hold the milk jug to their ears while you do the gentle zinging.

What You Say

Today I have a Zingy Thingy. *(Show your milk jug and Slinky apparatus.)* This setup will help us learn two verses with a lot of sound in them. Listen to Psalm 96:11, 12: "Let the heavens rejoice, let the earth be glad; let the sea resound, and all that is in it. Let the fields be jubilant, and everything in them; let all the trees of the forest sing for joy."

In two short verses we have the heavens rejoicing, the earth being glad, the seas resounding, the fields being jubilant, and the trees singing.

Mercy. Wonder what all those different noises would sound like when they come together? Especially those singing trees? Maybe that's where our Zingy Thingy comes in. Would somebody like to hold the milk jug in your hand? *(Select a volunteer.)* Okay, good. Hold the open end up to your ear. Get a good grip on the handle. Great, you are set.

Now I'll move over here and stretch out the Slinky. I'll gently move the Slinky up and down, maybe tap it with my finger, and you let me know what you hear. Okay? Here we go. *(Make a few different sounds—short, long, up, down, taps, etc.)* How did you like those sounds? Pretty neat, huh? How about another volunteer? *(And again.)*

So, who knows, when the heavens rejoice and the earth is glad, when the seas resound and the fields are jubilant, and when the trees sing, maybe it comes out like that—springy and zingy. One thing for sure, all those sounds are happy ones. And that's the lesson of the Zingy Thingy. Let's be happy in the Lord.

East to West, Least to Best

Psalm 103:12

As far as the east is from the west, so far has he removed our transgressions from us.

What's Gonna Happen

You're going to make two little boats from plastic containers.

The How Behind the Wow

In the bottom of one plastic container you will punch several nail holes. Putting this container on water, you'll find that it floats. Surface tension keeps the water from entering the holes. You will then place a small section of facial tissue into your boat. Capillary action will pull water through the holes in your boat and into the tissue. As soon as this process begins, there's no stopping. Your boat will continue filling with water till it sinks.

What You Need

2 sandwich-size plastic containers
Water
Paper towel
Scissors
#8 nail

Heat source (Sterno®, candle, etc.)
Large plastic tub or aquarium
Matches
Facial tissues
Permanent marker

What You Do

1. Use a match to light the Sterno or candle.
2. Fold the paper towel to hold the nail.
3. Heat the point of the nail for two or three minutes.
4. Turn *one* of the small tubs upside down. With the hot nail, begin punching holes in the tub bottom. You will have to return to the heat source often to keep the nail hot. Make some 25 holes spaced out evenly. Use the marker to write OUR BOAT on the side of this container. Leave the other small plastic container as it is, but write GOD'S BOAT on the side of it.
5. With the scissors, cut two squares from the facial tissues. Each square should *easily* fit in the bottoms of the plastic containers.
6. Fill the plastic tub or aquarium half full of water. Gently set the two plastic containers on the water. Both tubs will float.
7. Lay the two tissue cutouts into the bottoms of the containers. The tissue in the "holey tub" will instantly begin drawing in water. This will continue till the tub sinks.
8. You're good to go. Take all things for your talk. Be sure the tub with holes is good and dry or it may sink as soon as you put it in the H_2O.
9. Have two fresh tissue cutouts, of course.

What You Say

One of the best things of all about God is his forgiveness of things we do wrong. If we slip up and do something, say something, feel something that we shouldn't, we just need to go to God. There we tell him that we're sorry for what we did and ask him to forgive us. Psalm 103:12 says this about God's reaction to us: "As far as the east is from the west, so far has he removed our transgressions from us."

Pretty nice, huh? The east is a long ways from the west. That's how far away from us God has removed our sins. You might say that God helps float our boat throughout our life. That's what all of this is about that you see here. Look, I have a big tub *(aquarium)* with water in it. And I have two boats. *(Show the boats, bottoms and all.)* You'll notice one of the boats is in perfect shape. That'd be like God, for he is perfect. So I call this GOD'S BOAT. The other boat? Not so perfect. See those holes in the bottom? That'd be like us—made in God's image, but not perfect. I call this OUR BOAT.

But watch what happens when I put both boats into the water. *(Do this gently.)* Look, they both float. We might be tempted to think we don't need God's help in any way; that we're good to go on our own. Hey, we're floating, aren't we? That's all that matters.

Then God decides to do a little decorating in his boat, so he puts down some carpet. *(Place tissue square into GOD'S BOAT.)* We go, "Hmm, if he can do it, so can we. *(Put tissue into OUR BOAT.)* Then we take a deep breath; we're feeling good. We've got everything we need, we're cool, no prob—*yikes! (As boat sinks . . .)* What's happening here?

So, kids, when it comes to being perfect, there is only one perfect one. And that's God. Let's always sail in GOD'S BOAT with him.

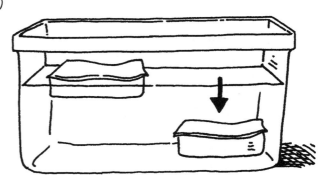

Riding the Wind

Psalm 104:3b

He makes the clouds his chariot and rides on the wings of the wind.

What's Gonna Happen

You're going to make some amazing clouds.

The How Behind the Wow

Dry ice is frozen carbon dioxide gas. When water is put on dry ice, a cloud is created. This cloud is made of both carbon dioxide gas and water vapor.

What You Need

Foam cooler
X-ACTO® knife #1
Duct tape
Permanent marker
Warm or hot water

1 package dryer vent expandable tubing
Dry ice
Glue
Hammer
Pitcher (2 quart or more)

What You Do

1. Because of carbon dioxide gas, do this demo in a well-vented area; outside would be best. Place the end of the dryer tubing onto the lid of the foam cooler. Trace around the tube. Use the knife to cut out this circle.
2. Insert an end of the tubing into the hole you cut. The tube should stick about an inch through the lid. Stretch tubing out about a yard.
3. Glue both sides of the lid to the tube. Duct tape when glue dries.
4. Purchase a block of dry ice at a grocery store. Preferably buy this the day of your talk; no sooner than the day before. The dry ice will be in a plastic bag. Pick it up by this bag. **Never touch the actual dry ice.** Put the block of dry ice in a paper grocery sack and set it into your cooler with the lid on.
5. We're not going to practice this demo, just trust that it will work.
6. Just before your talk, set the dry ice on concrete. While it's still in its plastic and paper bags, hit it several times with the hammer. Pour the chunks and pieces out of the bags into the cooler.
7. Have two to three quarts of warm or hot water in the pitcher. As you're ready to begin the demo part of the talk, select a child to help. He will carry the tubing; you'll carry the cooler. **Remember, you're making carbon dioxide gas. Don't let anyone breathe it, including you.** Pour the water into the cooler onto the dry ice; quickly put on the lid and walk your cloud back and forth before your admiring audience.
8. When done with the show, pour out the water. Allow dry ice to sublimate (turn back to gas) in the cooler.

What You Say

One of the things that makes Bible reading so enjoyable is the language of the Bible. This is especially true of the psalms. It seems that the words are always painting pictures for us. That is really good writing. Some of the best authors of all time were great at painting word pictures. This includes such famous authors as Mark Twain who wrote *Tom Sawyer* and Margaret Mitchell who wrote *Gone with the Wind.*

Our verse for today certainly paints a picture. It's Psalm 104:3 and it says, "He makes the clouds his chariot and rides on the wings of the wind." As you might imagine, the *he* in this case is God. Isn't that a cool picture? The clouds are God's chariot and he rides on the wind.

Today, I have for us a "riding on the clouds and wind" apparatus. And it's this cooler with a tube! Hmm. Whoever would think a cooler could be used to ride on the wind? We'll have to see. First, though, I need someone to help me. *(Select volunteer.)* You hold on to the tube end. I'm going to pour in water, then carry the cooler. Together we'll ride our cloud back and forth across the stage. We'll be on the wings of the wind. Sound good to you? Me too.

Okay, everybody, here we go. Psalm 104, verse 3 is on the way. The cloud is our chariot, and we're riding the wind. *(Pour in the water and off you go.)* What do y'all think? Have we made a cloud or what? *(Make sure the volunteer is off to the side of the cloud, as well as the other children.)* We're riding on the wings of the wind. Yee-haw!

(As cloud dies down . . .) Let's remember, kids, our God is an awesome God. The clouds are his chariot, and he rides on the wings of the wind.

WARM WATER

DRY ICE

Don't Take It Lion Down

Psalm 104:21
The lions roar for their prey and seek their food from God.

What's Gonna Happen
You will have everybody bend their middle finger down, then try to raise their ring finger. Not gonna happen.

The How Behind the Wow
Our middle and ring fingers are controlled by the same tendon. When the middle finger is bent down and under, the ring finger can't be lifted.

What You Need
Your hand
Any surface (table, floor, knee)

What You Do
1. First, identify the names of the four fingers with the kids:
   - First—pointer or index finger
   - Second—middle finger
   - Third—ring finger
   - Fourth—pinky finger
2. Try this yourself to see and feel how it works: Bend your middle finger all the way under; other three fingers remain up.
3. Place your hand on a surface, keeping the middle finger bent under. You will be resting on the second knuckle of the middle finger. The other three fingers will be extended forward. All of your fingers should be touching the surface.
4. Lift the thumb and pointer finger and pinch them back and forth together. This is the way lions normally chomp.
5. With the pointer finger back down, try to lift the ring finger to "chomp" with the thumb. Try hard. Real hard. Can't do it. This represents the way God shut the mouths of the lions the night Daniel was in the lions' den.

What You Say

I read a verse in the book of Psalms recently, and it made me think of one of the great stories in the Bible. I'm going to read the verse to you. I want you to see if you can tell me what story it reminded me of, okay? Good. Here's the verse. Psalm 104:21 says, "The lions roar for their prey and seek their food from God."

What story does that bring to mind? *(Accept answers.)* You are so right. Daniel and the lions' den. Here's the difference though. In our verse today, the lions roared. *(You can do a roar, if you'd like.)* Listen to what Daniel says about his lions in Daniel 6:22, "My God sent his angel, and he shut the mouths of the lions. They have not hurt me." Just for the fun of it, kids, try to roar like a lion with your mouth closed. Kind of hard to do, isn't it? Yeah, it is.

In honor of lions roaring and lions snoring, we've got a group participation thing today. First, I need to show you the names of your fingers. *(Hold 'em up and name them.)* This first finger is called the pointer finger. This next one, the long one, is our middle finger. The third one is known as the ring finger for obvious reasons. And the last one is our little finger, or pinky.

Here's what I want you to do. Bend just the middle finger down on one hand. Now place your hand on your knee, on the floor, on your lap, or on a chair. Be sure the middle finger stays bent under while the others are out in front of you. Try to do this: Raise the pointer finger and thumb. Bring them back and forth together. Can you do it? Yes, you can. This looks like the way lions chomp things.

Okay, everybody, pointer finger back down. This time, while keeping your middle finger bent under, raise your ring finger to chomp. Ready, go. Hey, come on. The lions are getting hungry. These are the ones in Daniel's lions' den. Come on, come on. Nope, can't do it. And that is the way it was with those lions. The angel shut the mouths of the lions. Daniel's life was spared and God performed another great miracle. It's one that we still talk about to this very day.

Working for Peanuts

Psalm 104:25
There is the sea, vast and spacious, teeming with creatures beyond number—living things both large and small.

What's Gonna Happen
You're going to stick your two index fingers into ice water. One finger will get *so* cold while the other one stays nice and warm.

The How Behind the Wow
Just as whales have blubber for warmth, your layer of warmth will be provided by peanut butter.

What You Need
Creamy peanut butter
Bowl
Butter knife
Thermos

Water
Ice
Paper towels

Caution: Before doing this demo, make sure no one is allergic to the smell of peanut butter.

What You Do
1. Fill the bowl three-fourths of the way with ice.
2. Add water to the three-fourths mark also.
3. Take the knife and use it to layer peanut butter *all* around one of your index fingers.
4. Stick both index fingers in the ice water. Check out the difference.
5. Use the paper towels to clean up.
6. This demo will be really fun if you allow one of the kids to do it. That way all you have to do is just add water and peanut butter.
7. Plan on starting your demo with water about halfway up in the bowl. Add ice from the thermos at the appropriate time in your talk. Have lots of paper towels for cleanup.

What You Say

As the creator, God cares for all of his creation. This, of course, includes us. But it also means that he cares for the animals of the forest and the creatures of the sea. There is a verse in the book of Psalms that refers to those sea creatures. It is Psalm 104:25, and it goes like this: "There is the sea, vast and spacious, teeming with creatures beyond number—living things both large and small."

Did you know that the largest animal on earth lives in the sea? It's the blue whale. It can be as much as 80 feet long. That's like turning an eight-story building on its side and putting it in the sea. That is big, isn't it?

And not only are whales big, they have a layer of fat to help keep them warm in those cold waters. You may have heard of this layer. It's called blubber. Between their size and their layer of insulation, the whales are truly living large.

So let's check out how that layer of blubber works. I just happen to have a bowl that's half full of water. I'll add ice to chill things down. How about one of you putting your two index fingers in that water? Anybody? *(Choose a volunteer.)* Way to step up and volunteer.

Before you do this we're going to give you a layer of protection on one of your fingers—protection in the form of this peanut butter. *(Lay it on thick.)* You are good to go. One finger from each hand. And you're off.

(After 20–30 seconds . . .) Can you tell the difference? Sure you can. Ready to take out your fingers? Good. See how protected your one finger was? That's the way blubber protects the whales. What a creation! Even more, what a Creator!

Great volunteer. How about a few paper towels for cleanup? *(Provide paper towels for cleanup.)*

Twist of Faith

Psalm 105:8
He remembers his covenant forever, the promise he made, for a thousand generations.

What's Gonna Happen
You're going to make one single cut on a strip of paper. In the process the strip will turn into two connected circles.

The How Behind the Wow
This really is a wow. A Möbius strip is a single strip of paper with a half-twist before connecting into a circle. This half-twist creates a strip of paper with only a top surface. For a much deeper explanation, go to Wikipedia®.

What You Need
Plain paper   Ruler
Pen or pencil   Scissors
Transparent tape

What You Do
1. Place the paper before you, with lengthwise facing top to bottom.
2. Use the ruler and pen to dot off four two-inch sections on the paper. Repeat these four dots across the bottom of the page.
3. Connect the dots with the ruler and pen to make four lines on the page. Cut along these lines with the scissors. Discard the last half-inch.
4. Lay two of the strips end to end with a one-inch overlap. Tape top and bottom to create a paper strip some 21 inches long.
5. At each end of this long paper strip, put a *T* for top.
6. Measure across this paper strip. As you'll recall, it's two inches wide. Make a mark 1½ inches from one edge. Repeat this in three more places. Again, use the ruler and pen to make a straight line along the dots.
7. Finally, with this strip, bring the ends around until they meet and overlap. The two *T's* will be facing upward. Tape the ends top and bottom so that you have a circle. On the 1½" line, make a small slit and start cutting, making two circles.
8. Repeat steps 4 and 5 with the other two strips of paper.
9. Again, you will measure 1½ inches across the strip. On this strip just put one dot and that's good. No more dots, no connecting lines.
10. Here's the key step: bring the two ends together. Just before taping them though, give one end a half-twist so that the *T* on that end is facing downward. Now tape the two ends together.
11. With the second circle, make a small slit and start cutting at the dot. You don't

have a line to follow, so keep the same distance from the near edge the whole time. When you're done, you'll have two connected circles.

12. For your demo, cut out four new strips of paper. Tape them into two of the longer strips. Draw lines one one; put dots on the other. However, you won't tape these strips into circles until you are doing your talk.

What You Say

Today we're going to talk about a big word in the Bible. The word is *covenant*. A covenant is a promise, especially a promise of God. When God made a promise in the Bible, it was a big deal. You may have heard the term *promised land.* The promise of the promised land came from a covenant God made with the Israelite people.

Do you think God forgets a covenant once he has made it? *(Accept answers.)* You are right. He remembers all of his covenants. Psalm 105:8 says that very thing, "He remembers his covenant forever, the promise he made, for a thousand generations."

God's covenants with his people remind me of these two strips of paper. *(Show the two long strips already taped together.)* I'm going to loop this first strip around and tape it into a circle. This circle represents no covenant with God. So it is, as time passes *(cut this circle into two separate halves),* there's no connection between the people and God.

This other strip, though, has a covenant twist with the Lord. Watch as I'm about to tape them together. I'm going to give this side a half-twist and now tape them. I'll cut this strip the same distance from the edge as the first one. So here I go.

(As you cut . . .) Wow, this one takes a lot more cutting. Seems to be paper everywhere. But I'm going to keep cutting. What do you think we'll have when I'm done? *(Not a rhetorical question; accept any answers.)* Mercy, I think I just passed where I started. I'm still cutting, though and now we're done. Look, two circles. And they're interlocked with each other. You see, when God makes a promise—a covenant—with us, that is so special. He's saying he wants to have a spiritual connection with us forever. His forever covenant meant so much to him that he sent his Son, Jesus, to die so it could happen. Now that's a covenant.

The Möbius strip is named after August Ferdinand Möbius.

Bob the Prophet

Psalm 105:15

"Do not touch my anointed ones; do my prophets no harm."

What's Gonna Happen

You're going to make a bobbing prophet out of a ping-pong ball.

The How Behind the Wow

The curved surface of the ping-pong ball, along with the weight of the clay, allows the prophet to continually bob back upright.

What You Need

Ping-pong ball
X-ACTO® knife
Craft stick
Scissors

Copy of prophet from this demo
Clay
Markers or crayons, if desired
Glue or tape

What You Do

1. Make a copy of the prophet from page 156. Color, if desired, and cut out.
2. Glue or tape the prophet to the craft stick. Be sure some of the craft stick is above the prophet and some of the stick is below.
3. Use the knife to cut the ping-pong ball in half. Go easy.
4. Fill one of the ping-pong ball halves with clay.
5. Stand Bob the Prophet up in the clay. Give the prophet a little push. It will tip over, then right itself over and over.
6. That's it.

What You Say

Psalm 105:15 says, "Do not touch my anointed ones; do my prophets no harm." There are a lot of things going on in your life, in my life, in everyone's life. Worrying about old-time prophets is not one of those things. They had their day; we have ours.

Except for this—we can learn something from the prophets. First of all, their lives were not easy. That is "not" with a capital *N*. They had to learn to bounce back from setbacks, get used to sparse meals and bare living conditions, travel in all kinds of weather, and, put up with the road rage—and every other kind of rage—of the citizens around them. All because the prophets told the truth about God.

Like I said, prophets had to learn how to bounce back. With that in mind, today I have my little prophet on a stick. He's a happy camper, isn't he? You know why? Because *(push prophet over, let him bounce around)* he's learned how to bounce back. Look, no matter which way I push him, he always lands right side up. He bobs back up. That's why I call our little buddy Bob the Prophet. Get it? He bobs back up, so his name is Bob.

Like Bob, you and I need to learn how to bob back up after we've had setbacks. It could be we've been let down by other people, or maybe somebody broke a promise. Maybe we didn't do so great on a test in school. Things always happen. The secret for us is to *(give prophet one last push)* keep trusting in God and to bob right back up. It not only works, it's kind of fun. Anybody want to bob the prophet?

F.R.O.G.

Psalm 105:30
Their land teemed with frogs, which went up into the bedrooms of their rulers.

What's Gonna Happen
You're going to make a hoppin' frog.

The How Behind the Wow
Origami is one of the how's behind this wow. The other is that folding the paper at the back adds a bit of spring action. This will enable you to make the frog hop.

What You Need
Plain paper or card stock paper
Markers

What You Do
1. Use the following step-by-step directions, as well as the illustrations on page 217, to make your frog.
2. Have the paper facing so that the length is vertical before you. Fold the top right corner down to the left-hand edge. This makes the paper look like a sail.
3. Open the paper back out. Now fold the top left corner down to the right-hand edge.
4. Open both folds out. Push in at the middle of each fold. Push toward the center. This makes the paper look somewhat like a house. Flatten these folds well.
5. You now have a triangle at the top of the page. Fold the bottom right of the triangle up toward the very top point of the triangle. Do the same with the bottom left of the triangle. You have just made the legs of the frog.
6. Fold the lower right side of the frog toward the central line. Do the same with the left side.
7. Turn your frog over. At the very back of the frog, fold the paper up about a half-inch. Make a second half-inch fold after this first fold. The second fold is in the downward direction. These two folds are known as accordion folds.
8. Draw eyes toward the front of your frog. You can also draw any other markings you'd like to have. Near the back, print "F.R.O.G."
9. Set your frog on a table. Push down at the very back of the frog, then release. Your frog will hop. Each push down equals another hop.
10. The card stock allows you to make a stronger, hoppier frog if you'd like.

What You Say

Today we're going to talk about the difference between the letters *e* and *a*. You all know about the word *(spell)* T-E-A-M. A team is a group of people working together to make something happen. Maybe it's a sports team, or a team at work, or even in church.

Then there is *teem*, spelled T-E-E-M. When something is teeming, it means it is just overflowing. Which brings us to Psalm 105:30, "Their land teemed with frogs, which went up into the bedrooms of their rulers."

This verse is talking about the plagues that Moses called down on the Egyptians. You may remember that one of those plagues was an overabundance of frogs. The land teemed with frogs so that there were

Frogs in the shade.
Frogs in the heat.
Frogs in the ponds.
Frogs on the street.

They hopped themselves up
to the top of Pharaoh's stairs.
No matter where he looked
there were frogs everywhere!

In honor of that team of frogs that teemed upon the land, I have my frog. *(Show frog.)* It's a good frog. See those letters—F.R.O.G.? They remind us to Fully Rely On God. I'll just set my happy little frog down on this *(table, floor)* and give it a little push downward. There it goes, hopping away.

And may that always be us as Christians—teaming up to teem across our land—fully relying on God as we go. *(Couple of last hops.)*

Find the FROG origami instructions on page 217 of this book or on the CD.

Wave on Wave

Psalm 107:25, 26b

For he spoke and stirred up a tempest that lifted high the waves. They mounted up to the heavens and went down to the depths.

What's Gonna Happen

You're going to use straws and a strip of elastic to make a wave machine.

The How Behind the Wow

In the physical universe there are two major, huge categories—matter and energy. Any material substance is matter. Energy is basically everything else—light, sound, heat, motion. Waves only carry energy, not matter. Your wave machine will visually show a ripple of energy.

What You Need

½" wide elastic strip   Straws
Hot glue gun and glue sticks   Tape
Yardstick   Pen
Scissors   Newspaper

What You Do

1. Use the yardstick to measure off and cut a five-foot length of the elastic.
2. Lay down and tape three pages of newspaper to the floor. The newspaper will keep glue off the floor. Place the elastic on the newspaper and tape each end down to the floor.
3. Starting at six inches from one end of the elastic strip, hot glue straws across the elastic. Glue straws crossways along the length of the elastic. The straws should be about an inch apart from each other. Stop gluing on straws at six inches from the other end of the elastic strip.
4. Take the elastic from the floor. Have someone hold an end of the elastic while you hold the opposite end. Gently stretch the elastic between the two of you. The straws should be horizontal to the floor.
5. Tap down on one side of the straws nearest you. You will see a ripple travel the length of the straws, and likely start back toward you.
6. Practice till you get the most effective waves that travel through the straws. You're there. I can pretty much promise you'll hit a home run with your wave machine.

What You Say

Hey, how many of you have seen ocean waves? *(Acknowledge all answers.)* That's great. The question for today is—what causes those waves? Does anybody know? *(They may or may not. We'll see. Accept all answers.)* Okay, good answers. Here's what it is. The thing that causes ocean waves is the wind. The wind also causes waves on a lake. The stronger the wind that blows, the larger the waves become.

Our verses today in Psalms are 107:25, 26, "For he spoke and stirred up a tempest that lifted high the waves. They mounted up to the heavens and went down to the depths." Those are some monster waves, aren't they? Up toward the heavens, then down to the depths.

The Bible says that God stirred up a tempest. From what we've said so far, does anybody think you know what a tempest is? *(Accept all answers.)* Yes, you're right. A tempest is a wind. And not just any ol' wind. The dictionary says a tempest is a violent wind. God made some mighty, mighty waves.

Today in honor of God stirring up the wind to create those giant waves, let's make a few waves. Instead of using water, though, I have waves of straw and elastic. *(Show your setup.)* Would one of you like to hold an end? Good. I'll hold this end. We'll stretch it out a bit and watch what happens when I tap down on the straws. *(Tap straws.)* How about that? Did everybody see that wave ripple all the way across and back? Check it out again. *(Second time.)* Now I'll let our volunteer tap the other end. Hey, great job. Waves all over the place.

So remember, everybody, when it comes to stirring up the wind to make gigantic waves, nobody can match the waves God makes. *(Make one last big wave.)* Why, his Spirit even makes great waves of love inside our heart.

Don't Stress, Just Bless

Psalm 109:17b
He found no pleasure in blessing—may it be far from him.

What's Gonna Happen
You will put water in a bottle, then try to pour the water out through a straw. It won't happen.

The How Behind the Wow
When you pour water from a jug, the bubbles you see and the *chug-chug-chug* you hear is air going in to take the place of the water that is leaving. If the air can't get in, the water has a hard time coming out. That's the case with this demo. Water will either barely come out in little sporadic spurts, or not at all.

What You Need
Small-mouth bottle
Water
Plastic tub

Straw
Clay
Food coloring

What You Do
1. Put 10 drops of food coloring in the empty bottle.
2. Fill the bottle with water.
3. Form clay around the straw. Do this around the center section of the straw. You may have to warm the clay so that it is pliable. Place the straw into the bottle. Seal both the straw and bottle opening well with the clay.
4. Turn the bottle over and let water flow into the plastic tub. Very little, if any, water will come out from around the seal. If water keeps flowing, work on the clay seal between the straw and bottle. Other things to consider:
   a. One-liter size bottles are better than two-liters.
   b. You may need to change the height (up or down) of the straw.
   c. If you're using plastic, don't accidentally squeeze the bottle.
5. Before your program, refill the bottle if necessary.
6. When all is perfect, you're ready to roll.

What You Say

In most of the psalms David is going a hundred miles an hour praising God with all his might. Which, if you stop and think about it, is not a bad way to spend our days. Today, however, David has a bad guy on his mind. He writes Psalm 109 to take out his frustration. In verse 17 he says about this unknown man, "He found no pleasure in blessing—may it be far from him."

In that little verse we see that David's enemy was never nice to anyone. He never blessed them with kindness or a prayer or a nice word. Wow, no wonder David was having trouble with the guy. So David says, "You haven't been kind to anyone. May kindness be far from you."

This brings up a thought. God loves to bless us, but he wants us to pass those blessings along to others. When God is kind to us, he wants us to show kindness. It's like a cycle—the more we bless, the more we'll receive. The more we receive, the more we can share with others.

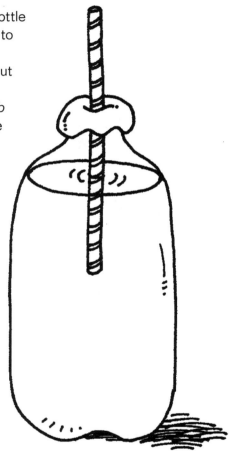

It all reminds me of this bottle with a straw in it. In the bottle is colored water that stands for God's blessings. He wants to pour out those good things on us, just like he did on David, and even like he wanted to on David's Psalm 109 enemy. But that enemy didn't want to bless others. His very actions stopped the flow from God. *(Turn bottle over above the tub to pour.)* See, nothing came out for the man. He could have turned his life around at any time and just had God's blessings flow all over him. But *(with bottle tipped over)* no. Nothing. Nada. Nope. An occasional trickle, but that does no more good than a single raindrop helps the desert.

(With bottle upright, remove straw and clay. Begin to pour water as you conclude . . .) So, kids, always have an attitude of gratitude toward God. And when it comes time for passing on the blessings, let's go with the flow.

Dial Me Up, Scotty

Psalm 113:3
From the rising of the sun to the place where it sets, the name of the LORD is to be praised.

What's Gonna Happen
You're going to "create" time with a sundial.

The How Behind the Wow
Sundials were some of the earliest timepieces. As the sun apparently "moved" from east to west through the sky, the shadow cast by the gnomon (*silent* g), or pin, kept time by the hour. Though we know today that the shadow's movement is because of the earth's rotation, we still use terms like *sunrise* and *sunset*.

What You Need
Corrugated cardboard

Scissors

Glue or tape

Photocopy of sundial pattern with this demo

Toothpick or wooden matchstick

Flashlight

What You Do
1. Make a copy of the sundial.
2. Cut out the sundial.
3. Cut a comparable piece of cardboard. Glue or tape the sundial to the cardboard.
4. Make a small hole at the "toothpick" site, where all the straight lines meet. Put a drop of glue on the hole. Stand the toothpick up in the hole. Allow the toothpick to dry standing straight up.
5. Place the sundial on the floor.
6. Stand next to the flat edge of the dial, near the right side. The right side would be as you are facing the sundial. Have the flashlight close enough to the sundial to overcome the room lights. When you turn on the flashlight and point it toward the toothpick, the shadow will fall on the morning hours (6:00 a.m. going up to 12 noon). Make the shadow fall on 6:00 a.m. As you slowly arc the flashlight to the left "across the sky," the shadow from the toothpick will move up through the morning hours. Keep arcing the light through the sky. The shadow will move past noon into the afternoon hours. Finally, you will turn the flashlight off when the shadow is at 6:00 p.m. Check it out.

What You Say

Listen to this verse in Psalm 113:3, "From the rising of the sun to the place where it sets, the name of the LORD is to be praised." Isn't that a great verse? It seems that the Bible is full of astronomy verses like that, and the Bible is full of praise.

So in honor of the "rising of the sun to the place where it sets" and in honor of praising God, I have today a sundial. *(Show sundial.)* What do you think? Let's check it out. This flat edge over here faces toward the sun. And here are the daylight hours, starting at six in the morning. *(Point out the six on the left side.)* Look, you can see where the hours go up to noon at the top. Then the hours drop back down on the right to six in the afternoon. And the toothpick in the center is the key. It casts a shadow from the sun.

Let's put our sundial on the floor. I've got a flashlight, and we'll let it be the sun. So here we go. *(Shine from lower right side so shadow is on 6:00 a.m.)* Remember, the verse says, "from the rising of the sun." Here's our rising sun. Now the day moves along. *(Start moving to your left so the shadow will move to the right.)* Now, it's nine and things are fine. Hey, that's a rhyme. Let's keep that up. Soon it's noon. Must be two in Kalamazoo. Now it's four in Singapore. Sakes alive, now it's five. It's six in the evening; time to be leaving. That was fun; now we're done.

Remember the point, everybody. From the rising of the sun to the place where it sets, the name of the Lord is to be what? *(Allow answers.)* That's right. Praised. Let's raise God's praise all our days.

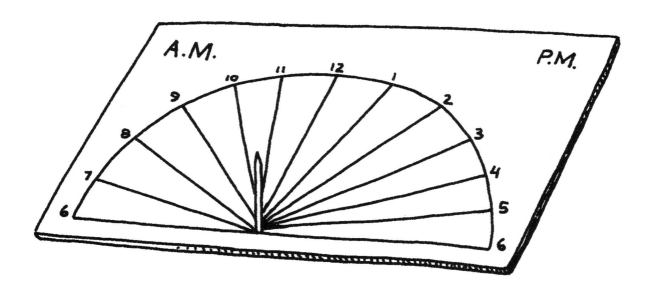

Gotta Hand It to You

Psalm 118:16
"The LORD's right hand is lifted high; the LORD's right hand has done mighty things!"

What's Gonna Happen
You will be able to use one hand to keep anyone from standing up. Actually, you will be able to do this with one finger. If you choose young volunteers, they may need their whole hand to make it work.

The How Behind the Wow
When people are sitting and want to stand, they must lean forward to shift their center of gravity over their feet. By pushing against their forehead with either your finger or hand, you can keep them from leaning forward. Therefore, they will be unable to stand.

What You Need
Chair

What You Do
1. Have your practice volunteer sit in the chair.
2. Ask the volunteer to stand. No problem.
3. After the volunteer is reseated for trial two, put your index finger on his or her forehead. Push against the forehead as the volunteer tries to stand a second time. Your push will keep the volunteer from being able to lean forward. Therefore the volunteer will be unable to stand.
4. You can have a child try this also, taking your place. The child can use his or her hand to push against someone who tries to stand.

What You Say

In the Bible, the word *hand* appears more than 700 times. How about that? More than 700 times, and many of those are talking about the mighty hand of God. For example, today's verse is Psalm 118:16. The word *hand* is in this verse twice. Listen closely. "The LORD's right hand is lifted high; the LORD's right hand has done mighty things!"

God's hand is mighty in all he does. For that matter, God made our hands pretty strong too. Do you know you can use just one finger to keep anyone from standing up? It's true. Check this out. Here's a chair. I need a volunteer to sit in the chair. Okay, great. Let's see if you can stand up. *(Allow the volunteer to stand.)* Good. No prob, Bob.

Now I'm going to use just one finger to keep you from standing up. Okay? Are you ready? Good, here we go. I'm going to just push right here against your forehead. *(Do this.)* Now try to stand up. Come on. Anytime now. See, there's no way for you to stand. My finger keeps you from leaning forward. And we all lean forward when we stand up. If we can't lean forward, we can't stand up. It's that simple.

So, if you think about it, my finger was powerful. Yours can do the same thing. Try it and you'll see. *(If you wish, let kids get in pairs and try this.)* If our fingers are so powerful that they can keep someone from standing up, then think how strong God's mighty right hand is. His hand is amazingly, tremendously, humongously, incredibly strong. And that's something that makes us all want to stand up and cheer. *(Do so!)*

By leveraging your finger against your partner's center of gravity, you can have a lot of power "in hand."

Pyramid of Prayer

Psalm 118:28
You are my God, and I will praise you; you are my God, and I will exalt you.

What's Gonna Happen
You're going to make a little pyramid, using foam cups and paint-stirring sticks.

The How Behind the Wow
Your pyramid should stand steady, since the base is wider and sturdier than the top, just like real, out-there-in-the-world structures need to be.

What You Need
10–8.5 oz. Styrofoam® cups
5 paint-stirring sticks
Hot glue gun and sticks (*not* high-temp gun)

What You Do
1. Plug in and heat up the glue gun.
2. Making the pyramid:
    a. Layer 1 (bottom)
       • Lay two paint-stirring sticks side by side with a half-inch gap between them.
       • On the sticks, glue four cups. The two middle cups are facing down; the two end cups facing up.
    b. Layer 2
       • Glue one stick flat over the Layer 1 cups.
       • On the stick, glue three cups. The middle cup should be facing up; the two end cups facing down.
    c. Layer 3
       • Glue a stick over Layer 2 cups.
       • On the stick, glue two cups facing down.
    d. Layer 4
       • Glue the last stick over Layer 3.
       • Glue on the stick just one cup, facing up.
3. Give everything time to dry and you're set.

What You Say

David, who wrote most of the psalms, has been called "a man after God's own heart." David was a man of prayer. Prayer is a great thing. This morning I have a structure to help us think about prayer. It's a Pyramid of Prayer. It can help you as you pray. It uses only 10 words, so you will be able to remember them. Here we go.

There are four cups on the bottom row. Those are a reminder about four words to start the prayer. Those four words are "You are my God." They are found in Psalm 118:28. The best way to start a prayer is to focus on God, not ourselves. What better way than to say to him, "You are my God."

The second row has three cups. Those are for three of the best-known words in the world. The words? "I love you." Let's say them to God, as well as to people we care about.

The two cups of the next row remind me of two words we always want to keep in our vocabulary, especially when we are talking with God. Those words are "Thank you." Think about how many wonderful things God has done for you and say "Thank you."

Finally, on top is one cup for the word "Please." That reminds me that the time to ask God for things is at the end of our prayer. Just a few of the "please" requests we can make of God are things like: please bless my parents, please forgive me, and please help me know your will for my life.

So do you have the Pyramid of Prayer in your mind? Remember, 4-3-2-1. *(As you go back through the prayer, start at the bottom.)*

4   You are my God.
3   I love you.
2   Thank you.
1   Please.

Those 10 words can help us talk with God every day. When we do, we'll be like David—someone who is a person "after God's own heart."

Things of Wonder

Psalm 119:18
Open my eyes that I may see wonderful things in your law.

What's Gonna Happen
You'll drop a seltzer tablet through oil into water, then get your *oohs* and *aahs*.

The How Behind the Wow
Oil is less dense than water. Also, oil and water don't mix. For these two reasons a layer of oil will sit atop a layer of water. Seltzer tablets don't react with oil, but they do react with water. The tablets will fall through the oil and explode into the water. Their foaming bubbles are lighter weight than both water and oil, so these bubbles will rise up into the oil.

What You Need
Clear glass (tall is good)   Water
Alka-Seltzer® tablets   Food coloring
Cooking oil

What You Do
1. Put two drops of food coloring in the bottom of the glass.
2. Fill the glass one-third of the way with water.
3. Tilt the glass and gently pour oil down the side of the glass (that would be the inside of the glass). Pour till the glass is mostly full.
4. Break the seltzer tablets in halves and fourths. Drop these into the glass of oil and water and let the show begin. You can continue dropping the seltzer pieces to keep the "wonders" bubbling up.
5. Start fresh for your talk with your glass already set up.
6. By the way, you can always supersize this demo in a vase or pitcher. Keep the same ratio of water to oil; little more food coloring, though.

What You Say

I'm going to start today by setting out this glass *(or super-size vase)*. It has colored water in the bottom with a layer of cooking oil on top. Looks neat, don't you think? Tell you what, it reminds me of a verse in the Bible. That verse is Psalm 119:18 which says, "Open my eyes that I may see wonderful things in your law." Let's imagine looking into that glass is like looking into God's Word. It's got layers of neat things for us.

The writer of Psalm 119 is asking God for something. He's asking God to open his, the writer's, eyes. The writer is not talking about the eyes he sees with, but the "eyes" of his understanding. That way he would appreciate the wonderful things in God's Word. Isn't that just the neatest idea—to ask God to open the eyes of our understanding? When he does, we'll go, "Whoa, what a verse I found today! Wow, that chapter is so cool! Hey, check out this story in the Bible!" We'll "see" things we haven't seen before.

In honor of opening our eyes, I want each of you to close your eyes just a second. Ready, and go. *(After five seconds . . .)* Okay, good. Now open your eyes and keep them on the glass. Remember, we're looking into God's Word. *(Begin dropping in the tablets.)* Hey, what do you think? Are you seeing wonderful things or what? *(They'll let you know.)*

Let's drop one last tablet, shall we? Would one of you like to do the honors? Great. *(As it bubbles up . . .)* So remember, my friends, there are always wonderful things in God's Word for us to see. Let's just ask him to open the eyes of our understanding. Okay? Okay.

LIGHTLY COLORED WATER

COOKING OIL

Life Preserver

Psalm 119:25, 37, 40

I am laid low in the dust; preserve my life according to your word. . . . Turn my eyes away from worthless things; preserve my life according to your word. . . . How I long for your precepts! In your righteousness preserve my life.

What's Gonna Happen

You will put lemon juice on some apple slices, keeping the slices fresh.

The How Behind the Wow

As soon as fruit is cut, oxygen in the air begins to react with the fruit. This oxidation turns the fruit brown. The acid in lemons helps slow the oxidation process down. Vinegar will also work, but you're going to be eating one of these apple slices. Not sure you'd want a vinegary-tasting apple.

What You Need

2 plates   Knife
Apple   Lemon

What You Do

1. Cut five slices of apple onto each plate. Also, slice the lemon.
2. Squeeze lemon juice onto the apple slices on one of the plates. Leave the five slices on the other plate as they are.
3. The longer you wait, the greater the difference will be in appearance between the two samples.
4. You will start fresh for your talk. Plan on doing the actual experiment about an hour before your talk. Put lemon juice all over your "lemon" apples. That way, by the time you speak, the two samples will already be noticeably different. Take the lemon too. Begin with the plates out of view.

What You Say

Psalm 119 has a phrase that pops up nine times. That phrase is, "Preserve my life." David put his life in God's hands, and he repeated his trust in God over and over. Check out Psalm 119 sometime and you'll see "Preserve my life" many times.

In honor of David's plea for God's protection I have these two plates of apples. *(Show both plates of apples.)* These slices of apples came from the same apple. They were all cut an hour ago. Can you tell a difference between them, though? Sure, you can. This one plate looks much fresher. And do you know why? I put a preserver on it.

Here's the "life preserver." *(Show lemon.)* I put lemon juice on these apple slices and the lemon juice preserved them. These brown slices didn't get any preservative. So, hey, when we are preserved, that's a good thing.

Best of all, the preserved apple still tastes good. The lemon juice just adds a little kick. Think I'll have a slice right now. Anyone like to join me? As we enjoy the way the lemon juice preserved the apple slices, we can appreciate the way God preserves and keeps our lives.

Promises, Promises

Psalm 119:41
May your unfailing love come to me, LORD,
your salvation, according to your promise.

What's Gonna Happen
You're going to make a liquid rainbow.

The How Behind the Wow
There are a couple of things going on here. For one, in your rainbow the liquids have different densities. They stack up with the densest (syrup) at the bottom. Also, for the short term the liquids don't mix. They're immiscible. That keeps them in separate layers. Food coloring gives the rainbow its colors.

What You Need
Tall, thin vase

Clear syrup

Glass with water

Food coloring pack

Water

Plastic wrap

5–9 oz. plastic glasses

2 plastic spoons

Glycerin (sold over the counter at pharmacies)

Cooking oil

Rubbing alcohol

What You Do
1. Mentally divide the vase into fifths. The vase I use is 7½ inches tall and about 1¾ inches in diameter.
2. Set out the five glasses. Pour them half full of the following liquids:

Glass #	Liquid	Food coloring	Stir
1	clear syrup	7 drops red	yes
2	glycerin	2 drops yellow	yes
3	water	3 drops green	no
4	cooking oil	no coloring	no
5	alcohol	3 drops blue	no

3. Stir food coloring into the syrup and glycerin. Soak spoons in the extra glass with H_2O.
4. For practice, just pour an inch or so of each liquid into the vase. This should leave you enough of each liquid for your demo.
5. Pour layer one—the red syrup—into the vase. Pour this straight down the vase so that the syrup doesn't get on the sides of the vase.
6. Beginning with layer two, the glycerin, pour all the layers down the side of the vase. You'll do this by tilting the vase. This keeps the liquids from mixing.

7. From bottom to top, in order, the liquids in your rainbow are: syrup, glycerin, water, cooking oil, alcohol.
8. After practice, clean the vase, spoons, and extra glass. Cover glasses with plastic wrap and store liquids in fridge till program. Alcohol evaporates; keep an eye on it.

What You Say

Promises are good things. If we make a promise to someone, we should try and do everything possible to keep that promise. And it works the other way around too. Other people should always try and keep their promises to us. Like I said, promises are good things.

With that in mind, I have a verse today from the book of Psalms. It is Psalm 119:41 and it says, "May your unfailing love come to me, LORD, your salvation, according to your promise." God is the greatest promise keeper of all time. Beginning with Noah, then to Abraham, on to Moses, David, Daniel, on and on—God always kept his promises. So when we read this verse, we know that God's unfailing love and salvation are coming our way.

One of the great signs of all times about God's promise is the rainbow. When Noah built the ark, God flooded the whole earth. After the flood, God promised that he would never flood the earth again. He then put a rainbow in the sky as a sign of his promise. So today I thought we'd make a rainbow in honor of one of God's earliest and best-known promises.

We'll make our rainbow out of liquids (show glasses), and we'll make it in this vase. First, I'll pour in the red. Here I go. (Pour syrup.) Our second layer will be the yellow. While I tilt the vase, would one of you like to pour it? Good. Okay, pour about as much as I did with the red. Great job. Let's get others of you to pour the green, clear, and blue. (Go through these. When finished, hold up the rainbow for all to see.) How about that? You all did a great job. You sure you haven't made rainbows before?

In conclusion, let's allow this rainbow to remind us of the truth of Psalm 119:41—God's unfailing love will always come our way.

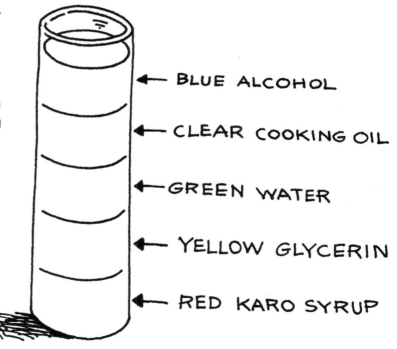

← BLUE ALCOHOL

← CLEAR COOKING OIL

← GREEN WATER

← YELLOW GLYCERIN

← RED KARO SYRUP

Sweeeet!

Psalm 119:47

For I delight in your commands because I love them.

What's Gonna Happen

You will float (or not) some candy bars.

The How Behind the Wow

When you first float the four candy bars in their wrappers, they all float because of trapped air within the wrappers. Three of the four are actually denser than water, so when taken out of their wrappers, these three all sink. The only one that floats outside of its wrapper is the 3 Musketeers. With a lot of air whipped into its interior, the bar is less dense than water.

What You Need

Clear plastic tub
2 each of the following candy bars: Hershey's®, Snickers®, 3 Musketeers®, Milky Way®
Water
Scissors
Paper towel

What You Do

1. A shoe box-size plastic tub will work for this demo. However, a 6.5 gallon storage-type tub will supersize the effect. Like most things, it will come down to what you have available.
2. If you plan on practicing this demo ahead of time, you will need two of each of the candy bars—one for practice, one for the real deal.
3. Fill your plastic container half-full of water.
4. With the wrappers still on, set the four candy bars on the water. All four of them stay afloat.
5. Use the scissors to cut the end off of each candy wrapper. Take the candy bars from the wrappers. Set the unwrapped candy bars on the paper towel.
6. Place the unwrapped candy bars into the water. This time, only the 3 Musketeers bar floats.
7. That's it. Dispose of the candy any way you think best. Start with wrapped bars for your talk.

What You Say

There are a lot of verses in the book of Psalms that talk about our relationship with God. *Relationship* is a big word that means how we get along with someone else. We have good relationships with our family, with our friends, and with our teachers. And we want to have a good relationship with God.

Now one of the key parts of having a good relationship with someone is trust. And trust comes from the truth. When we tell somebody something, it needs to be the truth. That goes for all of our relationships—family, friends, or God.

With that in mind, I have a verse for us today. It is Psalm 119:47. That verse says, "For I delight in your commands because I love them." We want that to be us—people who delight in God's Word. God wants that to be us too. Thing is, if we say it, let's mean it.

For your inspection today I have . . . *ta-dah* . . . a plastic tub half full of water. And I have these four candy bars. *(Show all.)* These candy bars represent us, and the tub of water represents God. That work for you? We say we delight in God's Word. You know what's good about delighting in God's Word—it helps us stay afloat in life.

So let's see if we float or sink. Remember, floating is a good thing. First, the Hershey's. What do you think? Will we sink or float? Here we go, and we floated. Let's go through the rest. *(When finished . . .)* Well, that was good. We all said we delighted in God's Word.

Did we mean it on the inside like we did on the outside? Hmm. One way to find out. *(Cut and remove wrappers.)* Let's try this again, shall we? *(Put in all four without wrappers. Save 3 Musketeers for last. When done . . .)* Whoa, that's a surprise. Not quite the same, huh? The point for us is this: let's be like this 3 Musketeers bar. It floated before, it floated after. It didn't change. Let's say what we mean and mean what we say. Especially when it comes to God and delighting in his Word. *(Hold up 3 Musketeers bar.)* Tell you what, when we do, it will be one sweeeet relationship.

Pouring Air

What's Gonna Happen
You will pour air from one glass to another.

The How Behind the Wow
Air can be poured in water. Since the air is less dense than the water, the air will pour up rather than down.

What You Need
Aquarium or clear plastic tub
2 plastic glasses
Blue food coloring

Water
Pitcher (optional)
Large spoon

What You Do
1. Fill the aquarium or tub half to two-thirds full of water. You may need the pitcher for this. Put enough blue food coloring in to make the water look slightly blue (not dark) in color. Stir with the spoon.
2. Submerge one of the glasses, tilting it as you push it underwater. This glass will fill with water. Hold it upside down somewhat near the surface of the water. All the water should remain in the glass.
3. Push the other glass straight down into the water. The air in the glass will keep water from entering. While keeping the glass pointing downward, move this second glass directly beneath the first glass.
4. Slowly tilt the bottom glass, the one filled with air. This will allow an air bubble to leave and immediately float upward in the water. If things are lined up correctly, the air bubble will rise into the upper glass. There the air bubble will displace some of the water in the upper glass.
5. You can continue this process until all the air in the lower glass has been poured into the upper glass. It's a neat visual effect.
6. For your demo, have the aquarium filled. You will put in food coloring as part of your talk.

What You Say

The word *rise* is our subject for today. The word *rise* appears more than 20 times in the book of Psalms. In many cases it is used to talk about David's enemies rising up against him. However, there's one time when *rise* is used in a totally different way. It's a way that causes me to think of this aquarium, the water, this blue food coloring, and these two glasses. *(Show all these things.)* Listen to what Psalm 119:62 says: "At midnight I rise to give you thanks for your righteous laws."

Psalm 119 is amazing. It stands alone in the Bible—and in the world in general—as a testament to God's Word. Thing is, we're not exactly sure who wrote Psalm 119. Some say a prophet named Ezra wrote it. Even more people think David wrote the psalm. Regardless of who wrote it, Psalm 119 is a true classic.

And verse 62, the one we're reading today? Right up there close to the top. The writer is saying that he rises at midnight to give thanks for God's Word. I wish that were me—getting up at midnight to thank God for his Word. Hmm, maybe it could be me. Or you. Here's how it might look.

First, I'll stir in a few drops of blue food coloring. *(Do this.)* I'll put in just enough drops to "blue up" our water and remind us we're talking about midnight. Next, I'll push a glass underwater and let it fill with water. I've got that. Now while keeping the first glass underwater, I'll push this second glass straight down so that the air keeps water from entering the glass. Pretty cool, don't you think? That bottom glass represents us, okay?

(With all lined up . . .) We're all set up and good to go. Watch as I tilt the bottom glass. That would be us, rising at midnight. *(Pour an air bubble or two.)* Can everybody see what's happening? Sure you can. We're rising at midnight and letting our thanks be lifted up to God. *(Finish up demo.)* And there you have it, my friends. We've lifted our thanks and praises to God our Father. So keep this in mind the next time you're up at midnight.

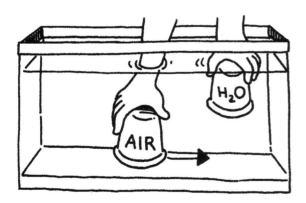

Bowled Over

Psalm 119:68a
You are good, and what you do is good.

What's Gonna Happen
You're going to put a bowling ball into a tub of water. It will float. You'll also put a can of Mountain Dew in the tub of water. The Mountain Dew will sink.

The How Behind the Wow
The density of water is 1 gram per milliliter. Objects will float if they have a density which is less than that of water. Lighter-weight bowling balls (such as children's bowling balls) fall into this category. The ball you use should weigh 10 pounds or less. The Mountain Dew sinks because its liquid weight, plus 46 grams of sugar, give it a density greater than 1 gram/milliliter.

What You Need
Water
Bowling ball (10 pounds or less—child's size will work well)
Can of Mountain Dew®
Medium to large clear plastic tub or aquarium

What You Do
1. Fill the tub or aquarium some two-thirds full of water.
2. Gently lower the bowling ball into the water. If it floats you're good to go. If not, borrow another one from your local bowling alley.
3. Check out the unopened can of Mountain Dew®, not diet. It will sink.
4. That's pretty much it. Let the waves and a strike roll.

What You Say

You may have heard the expression "sink or swim." It means we can either be successful or unsuccessful, positive or negative, do good or fall short. Sink or swim.

You and I want to have a good life, contribute to society, worship our Lord, and be good citizens. In short, we want to swim, not sink. Question is, who and what give us the best chance to have that kind of life? The "what" is a good education. Study hard in school or at home, pay attention to your teachers and parents, and be respectful. You will learn so much. The "who" is God. Following his path is always a good thing. A great verse in the Bible is Psalm 119:68. It talks about God and says, "You are good, and what you do is good." God really is good in all he does.

Today I have a tub of water. It is our "God-is-good, sink-or-swim" tub. I'm going to put two things into this tub—an unopened can of Mountain Dew and a bowling ball. Which one do you think will sink and which one will swim? *(Answers should be plentiful.)* Only one way to find out, right? That's what I always say.

So here we go. First, the Mountain Dew. *(Place can of soda in water.)* Surely that will flo—*Oops.* Or not. That leaves it up to the bowling ball. *(Set ball into tub.)* How about that? The ball floats. And there you have it. Sink or swim? I'd say we need to be like the bowling ball instead of the can of soda. Always keep in mind that God is good and the things he does are good. As we focus on his goodness, we'll always spiritually stay afloat.

The Big Dig

Psalm 119:72
The law from your mouth is more precious to me than thousands of pieces of silver and gold.

What's Gonna Happen

You will "mine some nuggets" out of a chocolate-chip cookie.

The How Behind the Wow

Elements and compounds are pure substances. Not so with mixtures. The ratio of parts can vary from mixture to mixture. Heterogeneous mixtures have parts that are easily recognizable from each other, like chocolate chips and cookie dough. On the other hand homogeneous mixtures look the same throughout, like homogenized milk. Hmm, milk and cookies—they should mix well together.

What You Need

Plate
Chocolate-chip cookies
Toothpicks

What You Do

1. Put a chocolate-chip cookie on the plate.
2. Use the toothpick to dig out four or five chocolate chips. Try to get faster as you go along.
3. That's it. Start with a fresh cookie for your talk. Have extra cookies for pass-arounds.

What You Say

Hi, there. Today we're going to do a little prospecting. In those old western shows there always seemed to be a prospector riding his donkey, searching for bright, shiny gold.

Today I've got a gold mine just full of nuggets. *(Show cookie on plate.)* You may have mined some of those nuggets in your own time. But did you ever use a pick? *(Show toothpick.)* Aha, got you there, didn't I? It's all good, though.

Before I start digging, let me read you a thought of David's about the value of gold. In Psalm 119:72 he says, "The law from your mouth is more precious to me than thousands of pieces of silver and gold." Did you get that, or did that shoot past you? David is saying God's Word is more precious—more valuable, more beautiful, more perfect—than pure gold. And this is from a man who would know. As king, he had his share of gold.

So keep that in mind as I start what I like to call "The Big Dig." *(Dig on in.)* And there's gold nugget number one. Look, here comes the second one. That was fast. I'll just set these two aside and keep prospecting. Having way too much fun to stop. *(Dig out a couple more.)*

I could go on and on, but I'd say those nuggets right there are enough to buy a new Hummer. Can anybody think of a quicker way to get the rest of the gold nuggets out of the gold mine? *(Accept all responses.)* I agree. Eating them would be a lot quicker. *(Time for pass-arounds.)* So everybody gets their own gold mine if—*if*—you will remember one thing: the words of God are more precious than gold, than much pure gold. Deal? Deal. Have a cookie on it.

Out to Launch

Psalm 119:120b
I stand in awe of your laws.

What's Gonna Happen
One bottle cap will drop straight down, while another bottle cap is launched outward—both from the same height and at the same time. They will hit the floor at the same time. Stay tuned if you didn't get a mental picture.

The How Behind the Wow
A projectile is an object that is launched without its own propulsion system. A rocket would not be a projectile; a thrown baseball would be. The forces acting on a projectile are the launching force and gravity. These act independently of each other, so that gravity works equally on a projectile and a vertically falling object. Thus, the two bottle caps land at the same time.

What You Need
Foam board

Ruler

2 bottle caps

Bible (optional)

Clay

Pushpin

Table

What You Do
1. Turn the ruler upside down.
2. Put the middle hole of the ruler an inch and a half from one edge of the foam board. This side of the foam board should extend three inches past the edge of a table. That is because your next steps are:
   a. to stick the pushpin through the middle hole of the ruler.
   b. to swivel the ruler so that one end is off of the board while the other end is farther onto the board.
3. Turn the bottle caps so that the open side is up. One bottle cap will sit atop the ruler. This bottle cap will be on the end of the ruler that is sticking off of the board. Place this cap an inch from the end of the ruler. You may need to put clay inside the caps for weight.
4. The second bottle cap will be beside the part of the ruler that is on the board. This cap will sit on the foam board near the side of the ruler that is closest to the edge of the foam board.
5. Swivel the ruler sharply by spinning the end that is off the table. Use your finger to pivot this end toward the foam board. This will do two things: it will flick the ruler from beneath the bottle cap, suspending the cap in space; and it will launch the bottle cap from off of the foam board. The two bottle caps will hit the floor at the

same time.

6. Practice a few times to get the routine down, then launch on.

What You Say

One hundred and seventy-six verses make up Psalm 119. More than 170 of these verses talk in some respect about God's Word, the Bible. The verses may use words like, *decrees, commands, statutes, laws,* or *precepts.* All of these are terms for God's Word. *(If you have a Bible handy, now would be a good time to hold it up.)*

One of my favorite verses in Psalm 119 is verse 120. I like it because of what it says; also, because it rhymes. The verse goes, "I stand in awe of your laws." Isn't that neat? God's laws are AWEsome.

Not only is God's Word awesome, God's laws of the physical universe are pretty cool too. Take the law of gravity, for instance. Without it, we'd be floating around in space. Instead, though, here we are, sitting on earth, getting ready to watch this little experiment. *(Show foam board with ruler in place.)*

Notice that I have a ruler that will spin around if I give it a push. On this end of the ruler, the outward end, I'm going to set a bottle cap. Over here in front of this end, I'll place another bottle cap. In just a moment I'll give the ruler a spin. The bottle cap sitting on this outer end will fall straight down, while the cap on the board will launch outward. Question is, which bottle cap will hit the floor first? You have three choices— the bottle cap falling straight down, the launched bottle cap, or they will tie. *(Accept and encourage all answers.)* All good ideas. Way to think.

Now let's find out, shall we? Watch closely. Here we go. *(And spin.)* Did you see that? They tied. Let's do it again. Watch closely. *(Set up and spin again.)* Same result. That's because gravity pulls all falling objects equally. This is just another reminder of what a great God we have and that we should always be in awe of his laws. Hey, want to see it one more time? *(Repeat.)* See, the law never changes. Nor does our God.

The Gift of a Lift

Psalm 121:1, 2

I lift up my eyes to the mountains—where does my help come from? My help comes from the LORD, the Maker of heaven and earth.

What's Gonna Happen

You will lift one end of a table—first without a lever, then with a lever.

The How Behind the Wow

The purpose of simple machines is to make work easier. They do this by increasing mechanical advantage. There are six kinds of simple machines. Levers are one of these. Any stick or bar can become a lever. All it needs is a place to pivot. This pivot place is called the fulcrum. Any of this taking you back to ninth-grade science?

What You Need

Chair

2 x 4 that is at least 5 feet long (other size boards will also work, but nothing smaller than a 1 x 4)

Table

What You Do

1. The table or desk that you're going to lift needs to have some weight, but not be massive.
2. Pick up just one end of the table. This is not with the lever—just you.
3. Position the chair a foot or so from the table end that you just lifted. The back of the chair needs to be the same as, or a bit taller than, the table.
4. Put one end of the 2 x 4 over the top of the chair and under the edge of the table. Push down on the other end of the 2 x 4. The table should be much easier to lift. The farther away you are from the fulcrum (chair back) when you push down on the lever, the easier it will be.
5. That's it. Take things with you for your talk, unless you already have a table and chair in the location.
6. If the size or strength of your kids fits this demo, you can have one of them do the lifting during your actual talk.

What You Say

There are two back-to-back verses in the book of Psalms. One of them asks a question; the other one answers the question. Those are verses one and two of Psalm 121. Verse one says, "I lift up my eyes to the mountains. Where does my help come from?" Hear that question? "Where does my help come from?" Verse two answers the question, "My help comes from the LORD, the Maker of heaven and earth."

Those are two neat verses, aren't they? Sometimes people think the verses are saying that our help comes from the mountains. But, no. Our help comes from the Lord. The mountains are good, but when it comes to help, God is great. The thing you, I, and everybody else needs to do is make sure that we're lifting our eyes high enough for our help. We don't want to stop at the mountains, but look all the way to God. The higher we lift our eyes, the easier the lifting is.

Here, I'll show you what I mean. See this table? It's got some weight to it; pretty heavy. But I'm going to lift it. *(Position yourself on one end.)* I won't be lifting all of it, just one end off of the floor. That will be like me lifting my eyes only to the mountains for help. *(Lift the table. If it is easy, add a little drama to the occasion.)* Wow, that was a struggle.

Now I'll lift my eyes all the way to the Lord for help. For that I'll use a chair and this board. You see, God is already sending help our way. *(Set all up.)* Now I'm way out at this far end on our little lever. I'll push down ever so easily, and look, the table just popped right up. Easy as pie.

So it is when we think of those two verses—the question and answer verses—let's remember that our help in this life comes from the Lord. He is surely number one; with him everything has more meaning and fun.

Oh, Boy. We've Got Joy!

Psalm 126:3
The LORD has done great things for us, and we are filled with joy.

What's Gonna Happen
You're going to make some super-duper, dry ice soap bubbles.

The How Behind the Wow
Dry ice is frozen carbon dioxide gas. When you pour water onto it, the ice begins to turn back to a vapor. This is termed sublimation. Pouring liquid soap into the container allows the escaping gas to make CO_2 soap bubbles.

What You Need
Dry ice   Water
Hammer   Joy® dishwashing liquid (has to be Joy®)
Tongs   Small pitcher
Small plastic glass   Larger pitcher
Aluminum pie pan

What You Do
1. Purchase a block of dry ice at a grocery store. Preferably buy this the day of your talk; no sooner than the day before. The dry ice will be in a plastic bag. Pick it up by this bag. **Never touch the actual dry ice.** Put the block of dry ice in a paper grocery sack and set it into a cooler with the lid on.
2. Set the plastic glass into the pie pan.
3. Put warm water in the larger pitcher.
4. Use the hammer to break the dry ice. (I always break the ice while it is still in the bag.) Open the bag and use tongs—**never your hands**—to pick up a piece or two of the dry ice. Put these into the glass.
5. Pour some of the warm water onto the dry ice. You'll immediately see vapors pouring out and down. CO_2 gas is heavier than air.
6. Squirt a small amount of the Joy dishwashing liquid onto the dry ice. Give it a few seconds. If bubbles don't begin rising out of the glass, then pour a little more of the warm water onto the dry ice.
7. Clean up well and you're ready to go. Don't pour the dry ice down the drain. You can put it outside away from people and pets. Or you can rinse it off and put it back in the cooler with the fresh dry ice. For your presentation, the smaller you hammer the pieces of dry ice, the more vapors you'll get when the water is poured. It will help if you hammer the dry ice ahead of time, scoop the pieces into the small pitcher, and have them ready in your cooler.

What You Say

One of the hallmarks of the Christian faith is joy. Pure and simple joy. Kids, joy is brighter than sunshine, splashier than fountains, taller than trees, and bigger than mountains.

It's been said many times that the key to joy is found in the spelling of the word itself. If we get those letters straight, we'll have the secret to joy. The *J* stands for "Jesus," the *O* for "others," and the *Y* for "yourself." Put Jesus first in your life, others second, and yourself last, and you are well on the way to climbing the JOY ladder.

In the book of Psalms, David sometimes had so much joy he couldn't contain himself. The joy just bubbled up and out of him. Listen to Psalm 126:3, "The LORD has done great things for us, and we are filled with joy."

So today, in honor of David, we're going to have a little bubblin' up joy. First, I'll set out this pie pan and glass. Now I'll reach into the cooler and get this scoop of good ol' dry ice. Don't get too close. Dry ice is *so* cold. We have to think about your eyes. I'll put the dry ice into the glass. Now I'll pour on a little warm water. Whoa, look at those vapors.

But the vapors are *flowing*, not bubbling. We need to add one more thing. *(Be sure the label on the Joy bottle is facing away from your audience.)* So I'll pour on a little dishwashing liquid. Now we have some bubbling up. There it goes. We definitely have *(turn bottle around)* the joy of the Lord. That's what David had in his day. Let's you and I have it in ours.

The Will to Build

Psalm 127:1a
Unless the LORD builds the house, the builders labor in vain.

What's Gonna Happen
You will shake up some glitter in two jars. In one jar, the glitter will quickly settle back to the bottom; in the other, the glitter will remain suspended.

The How Behind the Wow
Water is the liquid in the "settle to the bottom" jar. Mineral oil is the liquid in the "remain suspended" jar. Mineral oil is more viscous than water. Viscosity is resistance to flow, so the more viscous a liquid is, the thicker it is. This thickness enables the mineral oil to suspend the glitter particles.

What You Need
2 tall baby food jars   Water
Mineral oil   Colored glitter
Hammer, saw, etc. (optional)

What You Do
1. Clean out the baby food jars; soak and remove the labels.
2. Fill one of the jars three-fourths full of water and the other jar three-fourths full of mineral oil.
3. Sprinkle a large tablespoon of glitter into each jar.
4. Twist the lids on very tightly.
5. Turn each jar upside down and shake vigorously. Turn the jars right-side up and set on a table. The glitter quickly settles in the water. On the other hand, the mineral oil jar has glitter suspended throughout. The glitter can remain suspended for five minutes.
6. This demo can be supersized in pickle or other large jars.

What You Say

Have any of you ever used a hammer? What about a toy hammer? Maybe a real hammer? Hammers are for building things, aren't they? No doubt. Hammers, nails, saws. Carpenters use tools to build everything from storage sheds to big houses. *(Show tools, if you have them.)*

In the book of Psalms there is a verse that talks about building. That verse is Psalm 127:1. It says, "Unless the LORD builds the house, its builders labor in vain." One of the interesting things about that verse, about the whole psalm actually, is that the author is King Solomon. He knew something about great structures. Solomon's temple was one of the most amazing buildings in the ancient world.

In this verse, though, Solomon is saying that no matter how great the building is, unless God is involved, the building won't last. On another level, the verse is saying the same thing about each of our lives. As we build and construct the person that we are, we *really* need for God to be involved in that building. If he is, the building—our life—will have meaning and true importance. If we don't allow him to be involved, well . . .

So to show this I have these two baby food jars. *(Show these.)* Each of them contains liquid and glitter. Have you ever seen a snow globe? You shake them up and, *wheee!* Let's do that, shall we? *(Invert and shake well.)* There we go. Now *(right side up)*, let's watch the glitter. *(Point out the water jar.)* Check this one. See how the glitter is settling down? But look at this other one. How about that? The glitter is totally suspended.

Remember the verse, "Unless the LORD builds the house, it builders labor in vain." It's all about the house of our faith, isn't it? So looking at these two jars, which one would you say is lasting? Right. The glitter is there and not going anywhere. The other one? Already settled. Let's always allow God to help us build our life. *(Show mineral oil jar only.)* Remember those six words—"Unless the LORD builds the house."

Let's close with a prayer, shall we? Jesus, here are our lives. Please build them as only you know how. Thank you. Amen.

WATER   MINERAL OIL

March of the Starch

Psalm 128:1
Blessed are all who fear the LORD, who walk in obedience to him.

What's Gonna Happen
You will put iodine on several different foods.

The How Behind the Wow
Indicators change color in the presence of certain chemicals, thus indicating the presence of those chemicals. Iodine is a great indicator for starch. If a food contains no starch, a drop of iodine will remain its regular reddish-brown color. If you put a drop of iodine on a starchy food, however, the iodine instantly turns bluish black. You will be testing some of each food type—those with starch and those without—in this demo.

What You Need
Iodine	Flour
Salt	Medicine dropper
Apple	Potato
White plate (glass or plastic)	Sugar
Cracker	Knife
Spoon	Slice of white bread

What You Do
1. Set out the white plate.
2. Use the knife and spoon to make slices or small piles of apple, sugar, potato, salt, and flour on the plate.
3. Also on the plate, set a piece of bread and a cracker.
4. The iodine bottles I've seen come with a glass dauber. That won't work too well for this demo. It's better to buy a medicine dropper from a pharmacy and put the iodine on drop by drop. With this in mind, go around the plate putting drops of iodine onto each food. You will see it's easy to tell which foods contain starch and which don't.
   a. Iodine stays reddish-brown means food without starch.
   b. Iodine turns bluish black means food with starch.
5. Also, put a drop of iodine just on the plate itself. In your talk you will actually put this drop on first.
6. That's it. Start with all fresh samples of food for your talk.
7. **Caution:** Iodine is poisonous if taken orally in large amounts, so do not eat any of the food tested with iodine.

What You Say

One of the neat verses in the book of Psalms is Psalm 128:1. This verse says, "Blessed are all who fear the LORD, who walk in obedience to him."

Let's think about that for a moment. First of all, the thought here is not to fear God in the way we usually fear things. We're not supposed to be scared of God. Instead, fear in this case means to be in awe of God because of his majesty, his wonder, and his greatness. Once we get the hang of that we will want to walk in obedience to him as the verse says. Finally, if we do both of those things—stand in awe of God and walk in obedience to him—we will be blessed. That's a lot of information in one verse, isn't it?

Now you and I don't know who is doing these things and who isn't. It would be nice to think that everybody feared God and walked in obedience to him. But we just don't know. However, God does. He can easily see who is walking with him and who isn't. It reminds me of this iodine *(show bottle)* and the foods on this plate. *(Show and name foods.)*

Watch this. I'm going to put a drop of iodine on this white plate so you can see what color the iodine is. *(Do this.)* Can you see that iodine is reddish-brown in color? Sure, you can. Okay, now watch what happens when I put a drop or two on this little pile of flour. *(Do this.)* Whoa, did that iodine change color or what? It went from a reddish-brown color to bluish black. Iodine always does that when it is put on a food that contains starch.

With that in mind I'm going to go around the plate and see which of these foods contain starch and which don't, in much the same way God sees who is in awe of him and who isn't. We'll say that the foods with starch are those people who are in awe of God. Here we go. *(Start with apple and move on to bread, sugar, salt, cracker, and potato. Before each test, let kids hypothesize the outcome, depending on your time factor.)*

(When finished . . .) And there you go. Some of the foods had starch in them and some didn't. What you and I can't tell by looking, the iodine can tell by testing. Just like God can tell who really wants to know him better, be in awe of him, and walk in obedience to him. Let's always be those people, okay? Okay.

Special note: Kids may want to try this experiment at home with their parents' permission and supervision. Be sure to tell them that iodine is poisonous and that they should not eat any of the food they test with it.

The Karo Pharaoh

Psalm 135:9

He sent his signs and wonders into your midst,
Egypt, against Pharaoh and all his servants.

What's Gonna Happen

Prep time for this demo is two to three days. You will dissolve the shells off of two
eggs. You'll then put one of the eggs into Karo Syrup, the other into water.

The How Behind the Wow

First, egg shells have calcium in them. Vinegar is diluted acetic acid. The acid
dissolves the calcium in the egg shell, leaving the membrane below the shell exposed.
Secondly, osmosis is movement of water through a semipermeable membrane. When
a membrane egg is put into Karo Syrup, there is a higher concentration of water inside
the egg than out. So water moves out of the egg, through the membrane, and into the
syrup. Whew.

What You Need

2 uncooked eggs in their shells   2 plastic containers with lids (butter tubs, etc.)
Large spoon   Vinegar
Karo® Syrup   Water

What You Do

1. Put the eggs into one of the plastic containers.
2. Pour vinegar into the container, covering the eggs.
3. Put the lid on the container. Allow the container to sit for two days on a counter
    top. At the end of that time, check the eggs. The shells will either be dissolved
    or close to it. When the membranes are exposed, rinse the eggs with water to
    remove the vinegar smell. While rinsing, *gently* rub any of the remaining dissolved
    shell off of the eggs.
4. Pour out the vinegar, rinse out the container, and put in fresh water. Carefully
    place one egg into this water.
5. In the other container, put an inch or two of syrup. Carefully set the second egg
    into this container.
6. Check both containers a day later. Pretty big difference, huh? The water egg is
    large; the syrup egg shriveled up.
7. You're ready to go. The large spoon is for removing either or both eggs during your
    talk, should you want to do that. If so, take the water egg out first. You can hold it
    in your hand. Might think twice about passing it around though.
8. Have the bottle of syrup with you when doing the talk.

What You Say

Today I have something to show you. Actually, I have two or three somethings. The first is this bottle of syrup. It's called Karo Syrup. That name reminds me of the kings of Egypt. They were called pharaohs. See how it works? Karo. Pharaoh. Psalm 135:9 says, "He sent his signs and wonders into your midst, Egypt, against Pharaoh and all his servants."

The pharaohs had it made—big palaces, plenty of food, getting to boss everybody around. Think about those giant pyramids we can still see in Egypt. Those were built as burial sites for the pharaohs. Why, if we had been around back then, we would have loved getting a chance to hang out with the pharaohs. Or not. I'll show you what I mean.

I have two eggs with the shells dissolved off of them. It's true. I put them in vinegar and the vinegar dissolved the calcium of the shells. *(Carefully hold up egg from water.)* Underneath the shell is a membrane that still holds the egg together. Pretty neat, huh? After the vinegar dissolved the shell of this egg, I put the egg into water.

Like I said, though. I have two eggs. In this other container I put Karo Syrup to remind me of Ol' Pharaoh. There's also an unshelled egg in there with the syrup. If the water egg got as big as it did, I imagine the Karo Syrup egg will be huge, don't you? Let's check it out. I'll use this big spoon to just scoop it out. . . . Whoa, that's not big at all. The egg has shrunk way down. Maybe hanging out with the pharaohs wouldn't have been so great after all.

And that is the message today, kids. You're going to see lots of things in this life. You might think, "I have just *got* to have this, *got* to have that." Maybe, though, in the big picture you don't really *have* to have it. *(Carefully hold up water egg.)* Loving God and our family, working hard, and reading God's Word are things we really need for success in life. So let's always put God number one on our "Gotta Have" list.

(If you put the Karo egg into water, osmosis will fill the egg back up with water in about an hour. Then you've got a whole other talk about coming back to God, prodigal sons, etc.)

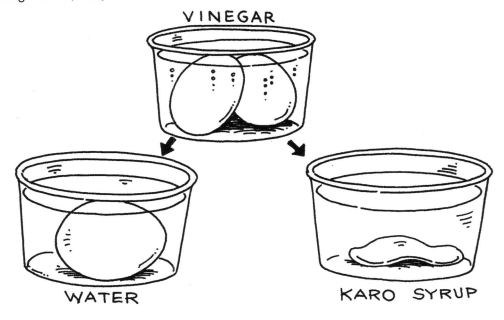

VINEGAR

WATER

KARO SYRUP

Bubblin' Up

Psalm 138:1a
I will praise you, LORD, with all my heart.

What's Gonna Happen
You're going to have a chemical reaction in one place. The results will show up in another place.

The How Behind the Wow
There are four phases of matter. The three with which we daily come into contact are solid, liquid, and gas. In some cases a solid and liquid can chemically combine to create a gas. That's what happens in this demo. The gas (carbon dioxide) moves along a tube till it bubbles up in a glass of water. (FYI: the forth phase is plasma.)

What You Need
Aquarium tubing (small diameter)   Alka-Seltzer® tablets
Scissors   Squeeze bottle with thin, cone-shaped top (sold
Water   in kitchenware areas at department stores)
Clear drinking glass

What You Do
1. Cut a two-foot length of aquarium tubing.
2. Fill the squeeze bottle half full of water. Leave the top off.
3. Fill the drinking glass with water.
4. Push one end of the tubing onto the cone at the top of the squeeze bottle. The tube should barely fit over the top of the cone. Place the other end of the tube into the glass of water.
5. Drop four seltzer tablets into the water of the squeeze bottle. Quickly screw the bottle into the top—not the top onto the bottle. You'll see why. (**Note:** Be sure to twist the squeeze bottle onto the top correctly. If you don't, all the carbon dioxide gas will fizz out around the lid instead of traveling through the tube.)
6. In a matter of moments you will see bubbles appearing in the glass of water. These will accelerate as more of the tablets dissolve, then the bubbles will gradually cease as the tablets are used up.
7. Reset all things for your talk.

What You Say

The word *praise* occurs more than 170 times in the book of Psalms. Many of the verses are similar to Psalm 138:1, which says, "I will praise you, O LORD, with all my heart." No matter what we say or do, there is no way we can praise God too much for his goodness to us. To me, I see our praises as bubbles that float up to the Lord, then burst right before him. Each bubble is filled with thanksgiving and gladness. The thing you and I have to always remember to do is raise the praise.

Not only was praise important to David and other people in the Old Testament, it was important to Jesus in the New Testament. You may recall the time Jesus was entering Jerusalem, riding on the back of a young colt. All along the path the people were praising Jesus. The Pharisees said to Jesus, "Would you have those people stop making all that racket?" Jesus answered, "I'll tell you what. If they don't praise me, the rocks will."

That's pretty huge, isn't it? The rocks will praise God if we don't praise him. I'm thinking I don't want a rock to have to do my praising for me. What about you? Right, you don't either. Good for you.

So with all this praising in mind, I have my Bubble Up bottle today. *(Show squeeze bottle containing water.)* This bottle represents us. What we're going to do is put a few tablets in here, twist the bottle onto the top, then see if our "praises" bubble up over where God is. God would be represented by this other glass of water. *(Show.)* Are you ready, then? Here we go. *(Drop tablets into water; twist on bottle firmly; make sure the other end of the tube is in the water glass.)*

Hey, how about all that bubbling way over there? That's just like our praises. We offer them here, then they bubble up before God in Heaven. No rocks are going to outdo us, are they? That's what I'm saying.

Above All Things

Psalm 138:2a
I will bow down toward your holy temple and will praise your name for your unfailing love and your faithfulness.

What's Gonna Happen
You're going to enlarge and copy the shape accompanying this demo. You will make two of the shapes, then cut them out. Though identical in size, one will appear larger than the other.

The How Behind the Wow
This is an optical illusion known as the Jastrow illusion, after its creator. The eye and brain compare the two curved surfaces nearest each other. The longer curve makes that shape always appear to be larger than the other.

What You Need
Photocopy of curved shape with this demo
Poster board
Marker
Scissors

What You Do
1. Make an enlarged copy of the crescent shape with this demo.
2. Cut out the shape. Use it to trace two of the shapes on the poster board.
3. Cut out the two poster board shapes. On one of the shapes, use the marker to horizontally write the word *NAME*. The shorter side of the curve will be at the right. On the other shape, horizontally write the word *LOVE*. Again, the shorter side of the curve is at the right. These two words—NAME and LOVE—should curve with the shape of the crescents.
4. Hold the shapes so that they are vertical and side by side. The long side of one shape will be near the short side of the other shape. The longer-side shape will appear larger. Swap the positions of the two shapes. Now the other appears larger. You can turn the shapes 90° and have the words read horizontally, just as you printed them. The illusion persists. Finally, stack them atop each other—identical in size.
5. That's it.

What You Say

(Start with shapes out of sight. You will show them one at a time later.) Hi, kids! Today's verse tells us about two very important characteristics of our God—his name and his love. Psalm 138:2 says, "I will bow down toward your holy temple and will praise your name for your unfailing love and your faithfulness."

I have written the characteristics on these two shapes. *(Hold shapes in either hand, far apart from each other.)* Looking at these shapes, which do you think is more important—God's NAME or his LOVE? *(Accept all answers.)* Great ideas. Let's find out more, shall we?

What I'm going to do is bring the two shapes toward each other until they are side by side. *(Do this so that NAME appears larger.)* How about that? All of you who said "God's Name" are so correct. Way to go.

However, as they say on TV, "But wait, there's more." Let's try switching the cards and see what happens. *(Do this.)* Whoa, check that out! Now "God's Love" is more important. How did that happen? Why, what if . . . *(switch cards back and forth, as you say)* God's Name is the big deal; no, his Love; now his Name; but wait . . .

(Finally, stack them atop each other.) Here is the real deal. They are exactly the same. God's name and his love are SO equally important in our lives. Kids, let's always chase God's heart of LOVE as we proclaim his majestic NAME.

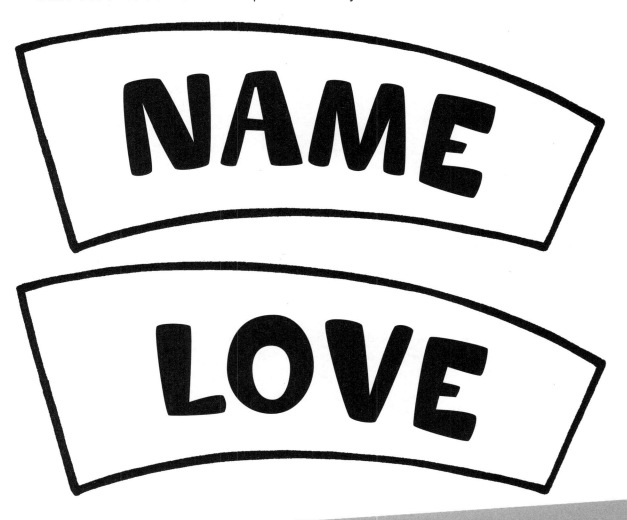

Talk About Fast

Psalm 139:10
Even there your hand will guide me, your right hand will hold me fast.

What's Gonna Happen
You're going to wham a drinking straw through a potato.

The How Behind the Wow
Trying to push the straw slowly through the potato doesn't work. The straw will go part way, then crumple. However, when you go fast, all is good. The straw blasts all the way through. The straw even ends up with a "potato fry" inside.

What You Need
2 potatoes
Non-flex drinking straws
Dowel rod ($^3/_{16}$" diameter)

What You Do
1. First of all, the plastic straws need to be the non-flex kind. Maybe you can pick up a few at a convenience store or fast-food restaurant. If you can find clear ones, that would be perfect.
2. Save one of the potatoes for the show. Practice on the other potato. If you're right handed, plan on holding the potato in your left hand. Hold the potato from the side, not underneath, especially on the fast part.
3. First, get a good grip on one of the straws and try to slowly push the straw through the potato. The straw will go a little ways, then bend.
4. Get a good grip on a fresh straw. While holding the potato in your left hand, wham down with the straw. You should be able to pierce all the way through the potato. Pull the straw back through the potato. A potato core will be inside the straw. If you've used a clear straw, this will be visible. Either way, whether clear or not, use the dowel rod to push the potato out of the straw.
5. That's it. Practice a few times to get perfect. Take a fresh potato, new straws, and dowel rod for your talk.
6. Note: If you can't get the straw to go through the potato even when going fast, then maybe you should:
   a. put your thumb over the back end of the straw as you wham downward.
   b. soak the potato in water ahead of time—maybe 30–45 minutes.
   c. try having someone else wham the straw while you do the talking.
7. Be sure to read over **What You Say** ahead of time.

What You Say

Hey, got a quick question for you today. Real Quick. When you hear the word *fast*, what do you think about? Someone running fast? That's good. Fast cars? Uh-huh. Speed, quickness, motion. All those things. That is certainly one use of the word *fast*.

But did you know there are at least two other ways to use the word *fast*? Both of them are in the Bible. We find one of those ways throughout the Bible when people fasted. Usually, this meant going without food for a period of time, maybe a day, maybe three days, or even longer. A word we use every day is related to this. If you take the word *breakfast* and separate it into two parts, you hear *break* and *fast*. When we eat in the morning we break, or end, our overnight fast. You don't have midnight snacks, do you?

The other way we use the word *fast* is found in Psalm 139:10. That verse says, "Your right hand will hold me fast." To be held fast is a good thing. God has got his strong grip on us. Maybe you've heard of safety pins being called fasteners. There you go—holding fast.

So the word *fast* is all over the place. Reminds me of this potato and straw. *(Show them.)* Our goal is to get the straw through the potato. Check this out. *(Barely grip the straw.)* If I don't hold the straw tight and fast, then when I push the straw against the potato, all that happens is that my hand slides down the straw. *(Do this.)* I've got to hold the straw fast.

Okay, I'm gripping tightly. But watch this. If I push slowly *(do this)*, the straw only goes a little way. Then it bends. After that, the straw is pretty much done. That's when I get a new straw, take a deep breath—are y'all ready for this?—and I ram the straw through the potato. *(Go for it.)* See, I had to hold it fast and go fast. Fast-fast. And with that I had success. Not only that *(push potato piece out with dowel rod)*, I can now fry up my potato chunk and break my fast.

Fast, fast, fast—all right there with a straw and potato. Who would have thought it? Let's always be thankful for the message of Psalm 139:10 that God's right hand holds us fast. And, with that, it's time for you to go. Just don't leave too fast.

Hey, It's in Our DNA

Psalm 139:13

For you created my inmost being; you knit me together in my mother's womb.

What's Gonna Happen

You will make a model of a part of a DNA molecule. Your materials will be Twizzlers and gumdrops. Pretty sweet DNA.

The How Behind the Wow

DNA has the appearance of a double-spiral ladder. The sides of the spiral ladder are sugar-phosphate molecules, whereas the rungs of the ladder are made of four bases. These are Adenine, Thymine, Guanine, and Cytosine. A and T always pair up, while G and C do likewise. It is the arrangement of these rung pairs on our 46 chromosomes that makes each of us the person we are.

What You Need

Twizzlers® Twists

Wax paper

2 gallon-size resealable plastic bags

Pack of gumdrops

Toothpicks

What You Do

1. Tear off and lay down a piece of wax paper. On the wax paper, put:
   a. 2 Twizzlers
   b. 8 toothpicks
   c. 4 each of four colors of gumdrops, maybe orange, green, yellow, and purple
2. Pair the four orange gumdrops with the four green ones; pair the four yellow gumdrops with the four purple ones.
3. Push an orange gumdrop onto a toothpick. Push a green gumdrop onto the other end of the same toothpick. Slide these together till they meet in the middle. Repeat this with all of the orange and green drops.
4. Repeat step 3 with the yellow and purple gumdrops. When finished, you will have eight rungs of your DNA ladder.
5. **Read all of this step before beginning.** Stick the ends of the toothpicks into the Twizzlers. (The Twizzlers are the sides of your DNA ladder.) Place the rungs in a random pattern. When done, you will want to give your ladder a half-twist in the middle. Therefore, it is *best to start your ladder rungs from either end.* The rungs don't need to touch each other, but do need to be fairly close. That way, when you are finished there will be nearly a two-inch gap in the middle. This gap will make it easy to twist your DNA ladder.

6. Make a second DNA model for comparison. Use the same color gumdrop pairs, but a different rung arrangement.
7. Store your DNA molecules in the plastic bag.

What You Say

Have you ever heard of DNA? Three little letters—*D, N, A.* DNA is made of chemicals arranged in tiny, tiny strands. It has often been called the molecule of life. Inside our bodies we have many cells. And in those cells are those ultra-teeny strands of living material called DNA. DNA looks something like this. *(Show one of your DNA models.)* This is a huge model of DNA. I used Twizzlers, toothpicks, and gumdrops to make our model.

Take a close look at the rungs—the crossways gumdrops—of the ladder. See how the purples are always with the yellows and the greens always with the oranges? Pretty neat, huh? Now watch what happens when I give the DNA a little twist. *(Give a half-twist.)* See how it spirals? That's the way our real DNA does. DNA looks cool.

Our DNA is what makes each of us unique and different. Check this out. *(Hold up second DNA model.)* See how the same colors still go together, but the arrangement is different? That's the way it is with us. We all have the same chemicals, but the rungs of the ladder are not the same. So some people have blonde hair while others have brown. Some have blue eyes, others green. And we could go on and on. DNA is incredible.

And who do you think made DNA in the first place? That is exactly right. God did. David didn't know about DNA, but he knew God was his creator. Listen to what he wrote in Psalm 139:13, "For you created my inmost being; you knit me together in my mother's womb." Yes, God did. He created David's inmost being, as well as ours. And the more we learn about DNA, the more we find out just what an amazing God we have. Hey, what can I say, it's in our DNA.

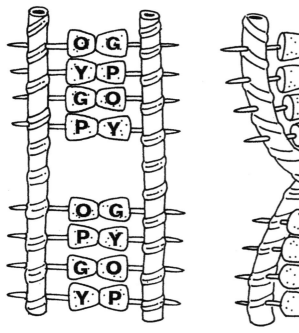

O = Orange
G = Green
Y = Yellow
P = Purple

Sands of the Seashore

Psalm 139:17, 18

How precious to me are your thoughts, God! How vast is the sum of them! Were I to count them, they would outnumber the grains of sand—when I awake, I am still with you.

What's Gonna Happen

You will test three materials—sand, water, and air—to determine which is best for blocking out sound.

The How Behind the Wow

Sound waves travel in a back-and-forth fashion, bumping the molecules through which they are passing. The more rigid and elastic the medium through which sound waves travel, the faster the sound travels. Generally speaking, sound travels fastest in solids, then liquids, and finally slowest in gases, such as air. Last thought: Depending on air temperature and elevation above sea level, the speed of sound in air is around 760 miles per hour. This speed is known as Mach One.

What You Need

Permanent marker	6 quart-size Ziploc® resealable plastic bags
Water	Sand
Cup	Sound source (radio, CD player, etc.)
Chair	Pan

What You Do

1. Use the permanent marker to print "AIR" on two of the bags, "WATER" on two bags, and "SAND" on two bags.
2. Put two to three cups of water in each of the water bags and zip shut.
3. Put two to three cups of sand in each of the sand bags and zip shut.
4. Barely unzip an end of the two air bags. Blow as much air as possible into the bags and zip them shut before the air can escape.
5. Turn your sound source to a moderate level. Stand some 8–10 feet away. As you listen to the sounds, press the two similar bags to your ears. The medium which conducts sound waves the slowest will basically block out the most sound.
6. The results you get in step 5 should match the info in **The How Behind the Wow.** Accordingly, you will hear the sound best with the sand, then the water, and least with the air. This is pretty much the opposite of what many people expect.
7. For your talk you need the six bags, the sound source, and the chair. It will simplify things if you take the bags in a large pan. You may need to refill the air bags before your talk.

What You Say

We've got a science experiment for you today. It's in honor of the Bible. Psalm 139, verses 17 and 18 say this, "How precious to me are your thoughts, God! How vast is the sum of them! Were I to count them, they would outnumber the grains of sand—when I awake, I am still with you."

Throughout the whole Bible there are several references to sand. Probably the most famous is the time that Jesus talked about the man who built his house on sand. Building a house on sand was not a good thing back then. Still not, I'm thinking. Now we have these verses from Psalm 139 that talk about God's thoughts being more numerous than the grains of sand. That's a lot of thoughts and a lot of sand.

So with sand in mind I have two bags of sand. *(Show these.)* But look what else I have. Since sand is a solid material, I thought I'd also have two bags of water and two bags of air. *(Show each.)* That way we've got three phases of matter—solid, liquid, and gas. And I have here a source of sound. Sound is not a phase of matter. Sound is a form of energy.

Here's the science experiment. One of you is going to sit in this chair *(have chair handy)* and listen to this sound source. *(Place the sound source you've chosen several feet away.)* I will stand behind you and hold these bags to your ears, one bag type at a time. I'll start with water, then go to air, and finally to sand. Which one does everyone think will block out the most sound? *(Encourage all the children to answer.)* Wow, great answers. Some think water, others sand, some air.

Let's find out, shall we? I'll turn on our radio *(do this)* not very loud, just so we can hear it well. Okay, here we go. Volunteer, try to remember how you hear the sounds each time, okay? First, the water bags. *(Listen for 15–20 seconds.)* That was our liquid. Now for the gas, which is air. *(Listen for 15–20 seconds.)* And finally, our solid, which is sand. *(Listen for 15–20 seconds.)*

There we are. What do you think? *(Here's hoping.)* Yes, you are absolutely right! The sound was noticeably quieter through the air bags. That's because sound waves travel slower through air than water and sand. In fact, of the three substances, sound travels the fastest through sand. Pretty cool, don't you think? God's thoughts are as numerous as sand, and just like sound waves, those thoughts come whizzing our way. God's thoughts are great things.

Twinkie, Twinkie, Little Pinky

Psalm 141:8a
But my eyes are fixed on you, Sovereign LORD.

What's Gonna Happen
You're going to put your pinky fingers together, end to end. Then you will stare through them as you slowly move your fingers apart. A little levitated finger—a "twinkie pinky"—will hover before your eyes.

The How Behind the Wow
This illusion is all about the "stare through." For example, focus on your fingers when you separate them, and all you see is, well, separation. Try it as you "stare through" your fingers though. This time you see a small hovering twinkie finger between your pinky fingers.

What You Need
Your hands and eyes

What You Do
1. At a distance of some five to six inches in front of your eyes, put the ends of your pinky fingers together, pointing at each other.
2. Stare through where the ends of the fingers meet.
3. Slowly separate the fingers. Between them you will see the optical illusion of a small levitated finger hovering in the air.
4. In your talk you will instruct all the kids on how to do this.

What You Say

I've got a verse for you today. It is Psalm 141:8 and it says, "But my eyes are fixed on you, Sovereign LORD." When we have our eyes—and our heart—fixed on God, good things happen in our world. The more people who do that, the better. When it comes down to it, you and I can make sure of only one person fixing their eyes on God, and that is ourselves. We can make sure we do that every day.

So today, in honor of fixing our eyes on God, I have a little eye-fixing activity for you. We're going to call this, "The Twinkie Pinky." What I want you to do is touch the ends of your pinky fingers together in front of your eyes. *(Have kids do this as you model for them.)* In just a minute I want you to look *through* your pinky fingers. You won't be looking at them, but *through* them.

Are you ready? Okay, good. Now barely move your pinky fingers apart from each other. Do you see the little twinkie finger hovering between your fingers? It's like a little bitty hot dog, isn't it? Move your fingers a little more apart. That little twinkie is hovering in midair.

And, here's the deal. You and I would have missed that if we hadn't had our eyes fixed on our fingers. Remember our verse? "But my eyes are fixed on you, Sovereign LORD." Think of what we might be missing if our eyes aren't fixed on God. We don't ever want to miss a thing, do we? No way. So let's always keep our eyes fixed on God.

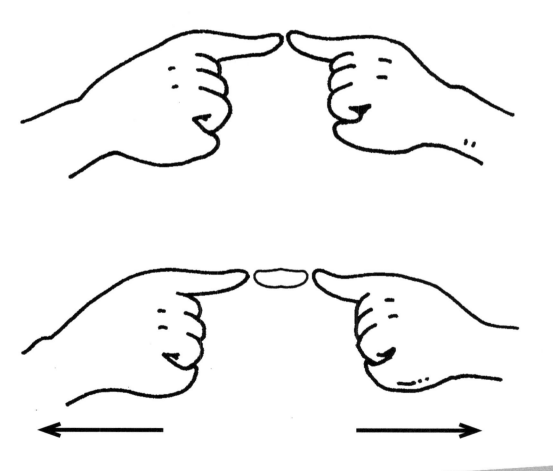

May the Butter Man Win

Psalm 143:10a
Teach me to do your will, for you are my God.

What's Gonna Happen
You will float a pat of butter in the middle of a bottle of water-alcohol.

The How Behind the Wow
Floating is positive buoyancy. Sinking is negative. Hovering in the middle then is neutral buoyancy. In water, butter floats. In alcohol, which is less dense than water, butter sinks. Get the right mix and butter hovers in the middle.

What You Need
Clear 2-liter bottle
Knife
Scissors
Rubbing alcohol
Ruler
2—9-oz. plastic glasses

Water
Cooler
Permanent marker
Stick of butter
Ice

What You Do
1. Use the scissors to remove the label from the two-liter bottle.
2. With the scissors, cut the top off of the bottle. Measure with the ruler so that this cut is four inches down from the top. This leaves a bottom section that is 8 inches tall. You will use this bottom part.
3. Label one plastic glass "W" for water; the other "A" for alcohol.
4. Pour 3.5 cups of water and 1 cup of rubbing alcohol into the bottle.
5. Refill each plastic cup with its respective liquid.
6. Cut a 1-inch pat of butter from the stick. I used Imperial® for this experiment. Place the pat of butter into the alcohol-water mix.
7. The butter will barely sink to the bottom. If so, add a bit more water until the butter begins to rise.
8. To keep the butter from rising all the way to the top, pour in a little rubbing alcohol. This causes the butter to slowly sink. Now it's a matter of going back and forth with small amounts of the liquids until the butter floats in the middle.
9. Remember: Add water, butter rises. Add alcohol, butter sinks.
10. Start fresh. Begin with water-alcohol mix already in the bottle. Have your two glasses full of their correct liquids. Keep a pat of butter on ice until super fun time. Wouldn't hurt to have extra water and alcohol on hand, just in case.

What You Say

There is a two-word phrase that is very important to us as Christians. I mean *very important*. That two-word phrase is, "God's will." We want to be in the center of God's will for our lives. That means we are living as he wants us to. It also means we are on the path through life that he has chosen for us. Being in the center of God's will is huge. God's will is not a new thing. Listen to Psalm 143:10: "Teach me to do your will, for you are my God." That was written maybe 3,000 years ago, but it is saying exactly the same thing as we say today . . . teach me to do your will, for you are my God.

To show you what it's like to be in the center of God's will, I have this two-liter bottle. *(Show.)* It looks like it has water in it, and it does. It also has some rubbing alcohol. That's the same thing I have in these two glasses. See the "W" and "A"— water and alcohol. In this cooler I have a pat of butter. *(Get this out.)* The bottle and the liquids are like God's will; the butter stands for us. Remember, we want to be in the center of God's will. So, here we go. *(Put pat of butter into bottle.)*

See how the butter barely sinks? I'll pour a little water in and watch what happens. There it goes, up toward the top. Now a little rubbing alcohol and it begins to sink. Pretty cool, huh? Now, if I can do this exactly right, the butter will float in the center. Yay! How about that? Scientists call that neutral buoyancy. You and I call it being in the center of God's will. And we know there is no better place to be than in the center of his will. Right? I'm saying.

(When finished with your talk, it's a good idea to remove the bottle from view. Chances are the butter will eventually float back to the top, losing some of the talk's effect.)

WATER ONLY

AFTER ALCOHOL IS ADDED

Rolling on Level Ground

Psalm 143:10b
May your good Spirit lead me on level ground.

What's Gonna Happen
You will make a ramp out of a three-ring binder. You'll then roll a full pop can and an empty pop can down your ramp. The contest here is to see which pop can—full or empty—rolls farther.

The How Behind the Wow
This demo needs to be done on a carpeted floor. The full pop can rolls faster down the ramp itself. However, once on the carpet its extra mass creates more friction. Therefore, the full can doesn't roll as far as the empty can does. Check it out. This demo can also be done with full and empty two-liter soda pop bottles. If you go the bottle route, you can also have a third bottle that is half full.

What You Need
3-ring binder

Empty soda pop can

Carpeted floor

Book

Full soda pop can

Coins or other markers (optional)

2-liter bottles (optional)

What You Do
1. Set the three-ring binder on the carpet. Put the book underneath the upper side of the ramp so cans will roll farther. The binder is now a ramp.
2. Place an empty pop can on its side at the top of the ramp. Let the can roll down the ramp and as far as it will go across the carpet. You can either leave the can where it stops, or mark its distance with a coin.
3. Roll a full can of pop down the ramp. Allow it to stay where it ends up, or mark it as you did the empty can. You'll find that the empty can rolled farther. Repeated tests will give the same results.
4. To supersize this demo, you can use two-liter pop bottles instead of soda cans.

What You Say

As David wrote the psalms he was always looking for God's guidance. Think about it. David was the king of Israel. Usually kings make a habit of telling other people what to do. David asked instead—asked God to guide him, lead him, watch over him. He was a king who knew who the real King was.

We have one of those verses today. It is Psalm 143:10 and it says, "May your good Spirit lead me on level ground." Level ground was a good thing in David's life. When the ground was level he and God were walking together. In another psalm he said, "You provide a broad path for my feet, so that my ankles do not give way." That would be Psalm 18:36. David didn't want his ankles to give way; he wanted level ground.

With that in mind, I have a "level ground" question for you today. Check out this floor around us. It's level, isn't it? Sure, it is. And I have this three-ring binder. *(Build ramp with binder and book.)* The binder is a ramp. What I thought we'd do is roll these two pop cans *(show)* down the ramp. They will roll down the ramp, then across the level floor, just like David's level ground.

First, however, before we start I have one small question. Which can do you think will roll farther—the empty can or the full can? *(Encourage all answers.)* Okay, some think the full can and some the empty. Anybody think they'll tie? Could be. Only one way to find out. So here we go. *(Empty can first.)* Hey, pretty good. Let's mark it. *(Do this.)* Now for our full can, and off we go. *(Roll full can.)* Oops, not so far. The empty can won.

That's kind of a neat experiment, don't you think? You can try it at home, kids. And you can change things to test—like maybe two-liter bottles instead of cans, and maybe a slick floor rather than carpet, and well, you'll think of things. Remember, however, the main point of our little experiment. David wanted to be led on level ground by God's Spirit. That is exactly what you and I want. Still today in the same way we want level ground all around. Roll on, my friends.

Smoke on the Mountain

Psalm 144:5
Part your heavens, LORD, and come down;
touch the mountains, so that they smoke.

What's Gonna Happen
You're going to fire up some flour.

The How Behind the Wow
Coming from wheat, flour is a grain-based product. Therefore it contains cellulose, which will burn. Being in particle size it also has much surface area. Picture a bar of soap. It doesn't have a lot of surface area because most of the soap is within the bar. If flour were like this it wouldn't ignite. Being in separate dust-like particles, though, gives it more surface area to combust.

What You Need
PVC pipe (4" diameter, 4' long)	Bible
Tapered candle	Clay
Flour	Plastic cup
5 x 8 index card	Matches
2 pie pans	Steak knife

What You Do
1. This demo can be done indoors but should be done in a room with tall ceilings. Also, don't perform it beneath smoke detectors.
2. Fold the index card in half lengthwise.
3. Pour a cup of flour into the index card.
4. Set the pie pan on the floor. Put a lemon-size ball of clay on the plate. Stand the candle up in the clay.
5. Light the candle and allow it to burn for 30 seconds.
6. Stand the PVC pipe over the candle.
7. Standing **at arm's length** from the pipe, sift flour from the index card down onto the candle flame. This part will take practice. Start off gradually, sifting downward and back-and-forth at the same time. Increase the amount of flour as you go. At some point the flour will ignite and three-foot flames will come out of the PVC pipe.
8. Just like that, it's over. Immediately put the pie pan on top of the PVC pipe to keep smoke from leaving the tube.
9. You'll find that you will need to use the knife from time to time to cut burnt flour off of the wick and top of the candle.
10. A photo of this demo is on the back cover of *Super Fun Science.*

What You Say

David was in fine form when he wrote Psalm 144. At the very first he talks about God being his rock, his fortress, and his shield. Then in verse five he adds a short prayer to his praises. In that verse he says, "Part your heavens, LORD, and come down; touch the mountains, so that they smoke." David wanted to see God's power, glory, and majesty. He wanted God to touch the mountains so that they smoke. That's quite a picture, isn't it?

Today, to help paint that picture, I have a candle and some flour. *(Show bag of flour.)* You've seen flour before. It is the white, powdery stuff your mom uses to make pie crusts and bread. Things like that.

Sometimes they say on TV, "Don't try this at home, kids." This is one of those times. Do not try this at home, kids. What I'm going to do is light the candle. After that I'll stand this piece of PVC pipe over it. The candle will keep burning inside the pipe. *(Do all this.)* Now I'll sift some flour down onto the candle flame. If we are fortunate we'll have a little fire come out of the top of the pipe: maybe six inches *(show this height)* or so.

(Get all things going and set up.) Okay, are you ready? In honor of Psalm 144:5, I call this demo today, "Smoke on the Mountain." Remember what that verse says, "Part your heavens, LORD, and come down; touch the mountains, so that they smoke." Let's see if we can have a little smoke on the mountain. *(And you're off.)*

(After flame has shot up . . .) I guess we got our six inches. Plus some. Think I'll just cover the tube with this pie pan. So if you ever see someone sifting flour down onto a candle flame inside a PVC pipe in a tall room with a high ceiling and faraway smoke detectors, just remember David and his prayer: "LORD . . . touch the mountains, so that they smoke."

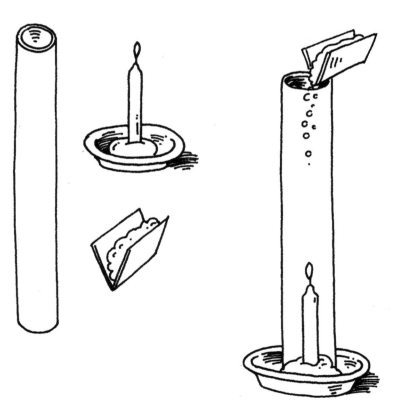

The Key to Victory

Psalm 144:9, 10a
I will sing a new song to you, my God. . . . to the One who gives victory to kings.

What's Gonna Happen
You will tie a key ring full of keys to one end of a string and a single key to the other end. The single key will support the whole ring.

The How Behind the Wow
As you can see in the illustration, the setup is suspended over a pencil. When you release the individual key, gravity pulls both ends equally. The greater mass of the ring of keys pulls the single key toward the pencil. This wraps the string around the pencil, which puts the brakes on the falling key ring.

What You Need
Single key

Key ring with 6–8 keys

Pencil or section of dowel rod

String

Scissors

What You Do
1. Cut a 15-inch length of string.
2. Tie one end of the string to the individual key. Tie the other end to the ring of keys.
3. Hold the pencil horizontally. Lay the string over the pencil. The key ring should be suspended near the pencil, while you hold the single key farther away from the pencil.
4. Let go of the single key. It will swing down and around the pencil, stopping the ring of keys from falling to the floor.

What You Say

Hello. Usually I have a verse from the book of Psalms to get us going. Not today, though. In fact, I've got a verse that's *not* in the Psalms. Think with me a minute. David wrote many of the 150 psalms we have. But do you know, not once in all of those psalms does he ever mention the time he killed Goliath the giant.

Everybody knows that story, right? The huge giant Goliath. David the shepherd boy. Size against youth; lies against truth. David used his sling and a river rock to whack the giant down. Still today we talk about Davids against Goliaths when underdogs face mighty foes.

You would think at least once in all the psalms he wrote, David would have said, "Y'all be strong like I was when I fought the giant," or "We have a huge challenge before us, like the time I faced Goliath," or "God will give us the victory, just as he gave to me the day I met Goliath in battle."

But no. David never brings it up. The closest we get are verses like Psalm 144:9, 10: "I will sing a new song to you, my God; . . . to the One who gives victory to kings." Notice that David doesn't bring up the Goliath battle. He does, however, say that God is the true key to all victories in this life.

So today I've got my key to victory. *(Show setup.)* Over here, many keys. That heavy key ring is like Goliath. On this side, just one key. Like little David. When I let the one key go, what's going to happen? *(Take all answers.)* Okay, all good answers. Let's find out, shall we? *(Drop the single key.)* Wow, look. The single key won the day. It stopped the whole key ring from falling. It's like David beating Goliath.

But that one key never says a word about how cool or strong or brave it is. It just does the job. And that's the way David was. He never brought up the Goliath story; never bragged on himself. That's a good lesson for us. When we do something big, let others talk about it. The sound will travel a lot farther that way. As for us, let's just stay focused on God. Because staying focused on God, my friends, is the key to victory in this life.

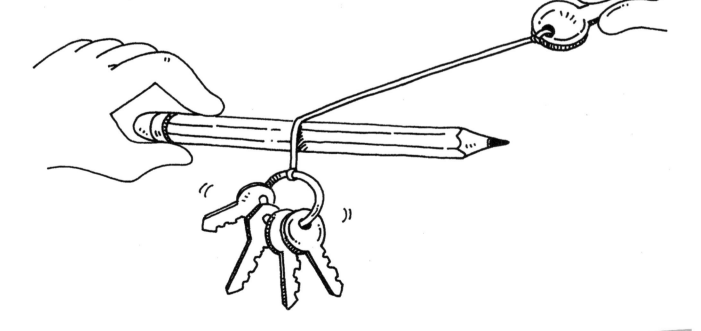

Wham!

Psalm 150:1, 3-5

Praise the LORD. Praise God in his sanctuary; praise him in his mighty heavens. . . . Praise him with the sounding of the trumpet, praise him with the harp and lyre, praise him with timbrel and dancing, praise him with the strings and pipe, praise him with the clash of cymbals, praise him with resounding cymbals.

What's Gonna Happen

You're going to wham down on foam cups.

The How Behind the Wow

The cup is sitting upside down on a table. You wham down on it with your flattened hand. The trapped air underneath is released with a major *wham*.

What You Need

Table
Styrofoam® cups, various sizes

What You Do

1. Place a small foam cup upside down on the table.
2. With your hand open and flat, wham down on the bottom of the cup. The trapped air beneath the cup is released with an explosive sound.
3. Try a variety of sizes of foam cups. You'll find that the larger cups make a larger sound.
4. That's it. You might plan on having the children, especially any younger ones, sit back a bit farther than normal.
5. Using two cups should be good for your talk. You might want an extra in case of a misfire.

What You Say

(Start with cups out of sight.) In all, there are 150 psalms. The last five psalms begin with the same three words: "Praise the Lord." Guess what three words each of those psalms end with. That's right: "Praise the Lord." Those three words are praise bookends for Psalms 146 through 150. And the very last psalm of all, number 150, is just full of praise to God. Psalm 150 is only six verses long, yet it has the word *praise* in it 13 times. That's more than two praises per verse.

If we look closer at Psalm 150, here are some of the ways we see the word *praise* used: Praise the Lord. Praise him with the trumpet. Praise him with the harp. Praise him with tambourines. Praise him with the clash of cymbals. Praise the Lord.

Wow, that is certainly a lot of praise. Did you notice how many musical instruments were used—the trumpet, harp, tambourines, and cymbals? They had a full-scale band praising God.

But you know, of all those instruments, nowhere did I see that they praised God with the *(show cup)* foam cup! Yes, indeed. If they could make praises with all those things, I can make my joyful noise with this foam cup. I'll show you what I mean. Everybody back up a little. It's gonna be loud. Foam really likes to join the party. Are you ready? Okay, here we go *(do it)* and *wham!* How about that? I think it fits right in with trumpets, harps, and cymbals, don't you? Sure it does.

The key here is to praise the Lord with whatever we have at hand. From a foam cup to a fishing rod, from a tambourine to a tricycle, from a blues harmonica to a football, let's just praise the Lord. Want to see it one last time? Or, should I say, hear it one last time? *(Wham second foam cup.)* There you go; let's just praise the Lord.

Have smaller children sit further away from where you do this demo. The "WHAMS" can be loud.

FROG Diagram

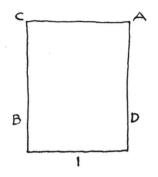

1

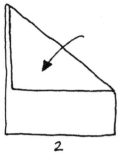

2

FOLD "A" TO "B."
OPEN BACK OUT.

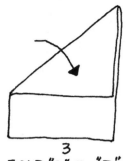

3

FOLD "C" TO "D."
OPEN BACK OUT

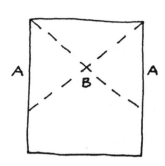

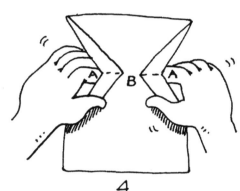

4

THUMBS ON TOP
FINGERS UNDERNEATH,
USE FINGERS TO PUSH EACH
"A" TOWARDS "B" AND FLATTEN.

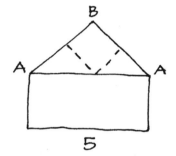

5

FOLD EACH "A"
UP TOWARD "B."

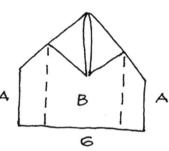

6

FOLD EACH "A"
IN TOWARD
MIDLINE "B."

6 (CONT.)

UNDERSIDE;
TURN OVER.

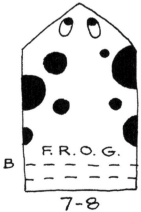

7-8

FOLD UP AT "A,"
THEN DOWN AT "B."

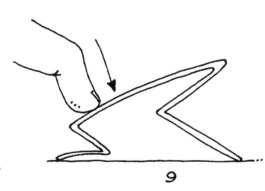

9

PUSH DOWN ON
THE BACK - FROG
WILL HOP.

Topical Index

All We Need
The Karo Pharaoh 193

Anger
Better Glad than Mad 19

Answer God's Call
Banana Hamma 123

Awe of God's Creation
From Mars to the Stars. 29
Blue Who? 31

Balanced Life
Park Your Marker 109

Be Like God
Be Like the One You Like 73

Be Still
Soft Pop 93

Blessings
God Is Good All the Time 63
Don't Stress, Just Bless 161

Boast About God
Disappearing Engineering 91

Clean Heart
The Circle Won't Be Broken 101

Delight in the Lord
The Air up There 79
Steppin' Out 81

Focus on God
Bowl and Arrow 51
Deep Calls to Deep 89
Fun and Done 133
Twinkie, Twinkie, Little Pinky 205
The Key to Victory 213

God Cares for His Creation
Working for Peanuts 151

God Controls Nature
Slo-Mo Flow 127
Riding the Wind 147
Don't Take It Lion Down 149
Wave on Wave 159

God Forgives
Time to Wash Up 99
East to West, Least to Best 145

God Hears Us
Now Hear This 17
Blur and a Whir 85

God Helps Us
The Gift of a Lift 185
The Will to Build 189
Talk About Fast 199

God Is Always with Us
His Grip Won't Slip 119

God Is Eternal
Chair Spin Curve 97

God Is Everywhere
Air Chair 95

God Is Good
Bowled Over 179

God Is Our Light
Be Brave in the Cave 21

God Is Our Shelter
Shelter in the Storm 103

God Is Our Strength
Getting in Shape 61

God Is Steady
Standing for the Lord 65

God Is Strong
Gotta Hand It to You 165

God Keeps His Promises
Twist of Faith 153

God Made Us
Hey, It's in Our DNA 201

God Provides
It's Raining Grain 129

God's Goodness
Spectacular Binoculars 71

God's Guidance
Going Green 57

God's Laws
Out to Launch 183

God's Love
May "Eye" Help You? 39
Falling in Love 53
As High as the Sky 75
Mountains of Fountains 77
Meet in the Middle 135
Promises, Promises 173

God's Power
Smoke on the Mountain 211

God's Protection
Strainer Things Have Happened . . . 15
Life Preserver 171

God's Thoughts
Sands of the Seashore 203

God's Will
May the Butter Man Win 207

God's Word
Color My World 59
The Big Dig 181
Things of Wonder 169
Sweeeet! 175

Heart for God
Penny for Your Thoughts 131

Inspiration
The Domino Effect 87

Joy
Oh, Boy. We've Got Joy! 187

Lean on God
Leaning on Jesus 107

Level Ground
Rolling on Level Ground 209

Ministers for God
But Will It Fly? 117

Nature Glorifies God
Star-Spangled Angle 45
Zingy Thingy 143

Near to God
Near and Dear 121

Obey God
Lettuce Be Strong 125
March of the Starch 191

Obstacles
Chase the Taste 69

Pain and Suffering
Bendable Bones 23

Praise God
High and Lifted Up 25
Did You See What I Saw? 27
The Choir Has the Fire 33
Dial Me Up, Scotty 163
Pyramid of Prayer 167
Pouring Air 177
Bubblin' Up 195
Above All Things 197
Wham! 215

Pride
Wind Tunnel in a Funnel 35

Produce Fruit for the Lord
Floatin' Fruit 11

Pure Heart
Clean Pure Through 55

Rely on God
F.R.O.G. 157

Restoration
Hooping It Up 49

Scripture Memory
Whack-a-Stack 47

Spend Time with God
Where Did the Song Go Wrong? . . 137
Deep and Wide 139

Stand Firm
The Chaff's in a Draft 13

Stay Close to God
Having a Ball 37

Tell Others About God
Spring into Missions 113

Temptation
I'm Predicting It's Addicting 9

Thirst for God
But First, the Thirst 111

Trust
Trust Is a Must 105
Don't Mope over the Soap 141
Bob the Prophet 155

Wait on the Lord
Weight for the Lord 83

Weather
   Lightning
   Static in the Attic 43
   Snow
   Diaper Diamonds 115
   Wind
   Wind-Wind Situation 41

Work Together
What's Up with the Cups? 67

Your First Lesson is FREE!

Why choose Heartshaper®?

HeartShaper® children's Sunday school curriculum
introduces children ages infant to preteen to God,
His Son, His Word, and His church.

♥ Flexible ♥ Fully resourced ♥ Interactive

♥ Age appropriate ♥ Multisensory ♥ Easy to use

**Download your FREE lesson
and review the
Scope & Sequence today!**

Visit HeartShaper.com or call 800-543-1353

Standard®
PUBLISHING
Bringing The Word to Life

"No one taught me that the church bulletin is the absolute worst place to recruit volunteers."

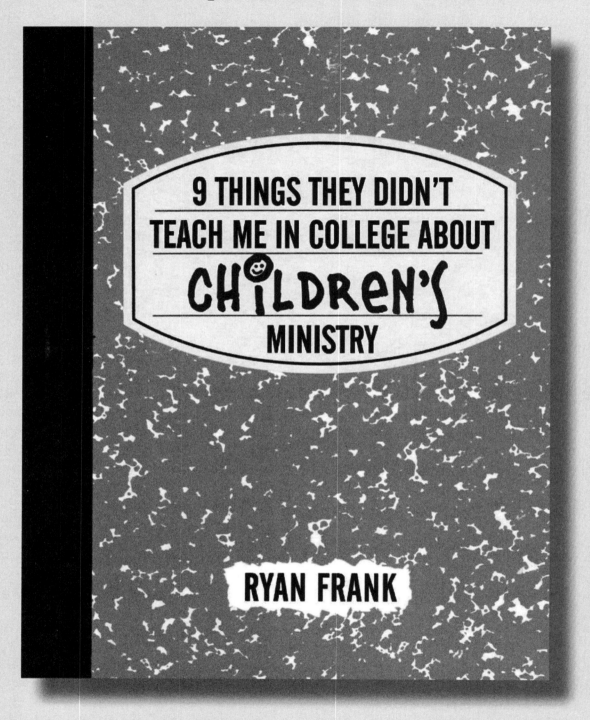

Find practical advice, inspiring stories, and interesting interviews with others involved in children's ministry.

A great resource for children's ministry leaders!